WHY BE GOOD?

David B. Smith

REVIEW AND HERALD® PUBLISHING ASSOCIATION
HAGERSTOWN, MD 21740

This book was
Edited by Gerald Wheeler
Cover design by Helcio Deslandes
Typeset: 11/12.5 Berkley Book

PRINTED IN U.S.A.

00 99 98 97 96   10 9 8 7 6 5 4 3 2 1

R&H Cataloging Service
Smith, David B.
    Why be good?

    1. Christian life.   2. Religious life.   3. Obedience
(Theology).   4. Good works (Theology).   I. Title.

                248.4

ISBN 0-8280-1068-4

Contents

A few months ago I got another traffic ticket. I say "another" because I just now realized that in the last book I wrote, *Watching the War*, I described a speeding ticket I received and the moral lessons I could learn from the $45 fine, plus traffic school. Now I get a new citation just as I start another manuscript. I'm starting to think I should either stop writing books or slow down my driving a little bit.

Anyway, this one was for rolling through a stop sign . . . on my way to church. I mean, I barely rolled through it—and I was on the Lord's business. And it was the Sabbath before Easter. I tried to explain that it was against my religion to receive a citation on Sabbath, but that did not matter to the police officer. "Here you are, Mr. Smith. Sign here. And have a nice day." Right.

Sabbath was ruined, of course. Then the bill came and destroyed my whole life. *A hundred thirty-eight bucks!* Some Republican in Sacramento is bumping up these fines at approximately 900 times the rate of inflation. Plus traffic school again.

I finally dragged myself down to traffic school on the two hottest June evenings in California's history. Me in a suit, of course . . . and then I discovered I was the oldest person in attendance. The average

age of the other attendees was approximately 16 years and 2 weeks. A bunch of pimply-faced children! Most of them sat in the sweaty darkness playing Nintendo games during the drunk-driving crash movies.

As I sat there and took the same dumb "Trick Question Rules of the Road" test for the second time, an eternal truth suddenly hit me: Obedience certainly has some great advantages.

That may not be a breakthrough thought to you, but it brings one of the great debates in Christendom to the center stage: Why Be Good? As Philip Yancey queried in a *Christianity Today* article by that same title, why should we strive to be "just as God wants" when He accepts me "just as I am"? If we accept the Protestant credo that our good deeds don't merit salvation, then why do we strive for goodness? Why obey the speed laws if someone else will pay my fines for me?

As I sat in the sweltering classroom and watched Sergeant Snooze endlessly diagram legal turns onto a one-way street, more and more benefits to goodness began to flicker in my mind. What follows in this book is what I came up with.

I'd like to thank the very kind "young adults" group at a Wisconsin Adventist camp meeting who sat in more sweltering heat and nodded their encouragement as I shared these topics with them. Especially the woman who brought me a 7-Up at the end.

CHAPTER ONE

The Conversion of Arnold Becker

A number of years ago I got into a vicious screaming match with my friend Chris Blake. Chris is a former editor of *Insight* magazine and now on the faculty at Union College in Lincoln, Nebraska, so he is a reasonably clear-thinking adult. At the time of this encounter, he and I were fellow teachers at an Adventist junior academy in Arroyo Grande, California.

The debate, ironically, involved $3. Three tattered dollar bills passed back and forth between us. Now, it's not what you'd expect. He was insisting that they were mine, and I was equally convinced that it was his money and that he should shut up and take it. I mean, neither one of us was going to keep that money when it belonged to the other person. No way.

The tirade grew to unbelievable proportions in both volume and intensity. "Blake, would you stop being such a stupid fathead and take this money and go home?" I screamed at him, my fists clenched and the veins in my neck standing out. (It really was his money, of course.) He responded in a very noisy and immature fashion until I was sure the mobile home park sheriff was going to come by with a shotgun and evict us both.

At last I took those three sweat-drenched bills and walked out of my house to where his car was parked. With a gesture of finality, I flung them into the back seat and stalked back into the living room. "There!" I bellowed. "That's the end of it. Don't come here again if you're going to act like such a baby. That's your money, and you know it."

Whew!

I really don't like to tell stories that make Chris look bad. I only do so to illustrate an eternal truth: **Humanity hates to get something undeserved. The idea of "grace" is absolute torture to most of us.**

Have you ever fought over a dinner check . . . trying to take it? I've seen people become almost apoplectic. "No, *I've* got it!" "Oh, no, I insist!" "You got it the last time." "Would you let go of that before I kill you?" Accepting grace—unmerited favor—is painful.

(By the way, several weeks after the embarrassing Blake episode, I was rummaging around in my refrigerator for something, and happened to look inside a seldom-used butter dish. Lying there in the mold were those same three dollar bills. I swear I don't know how he did it. But Chris, if you're reading this, go outside and look under the third flowerpot in your back yard . . .)

A while ago, while staying in Portland on official business, I somehow got assigned to a hotel suite. No additional charge, mind you. For three lovely days I soaked in the Jacuzzi, munched the free chocolates they left on my pillow, and generally felt quite pleased with myself.

The suite had *two* enormous color TV sets, and I really felt that I should watch both of them all I could while this fluke of fancy living continued. So I skipped meetings and shuttled back and forth between the living room and the bedroom so I could absorb all the luxurious ambience possible.

One day I made a chance remark to a hotel staffer about my very temperate love for cheesecake. That evening two huge slices of the dessert waited for me at my bedside. *This is heaven,* I thought to myself.

And yet it wasn't. I don't know if you will understand this, but after a while the suite life was not so sweet after all. I didn't really deserve to be there. After all, I wasn't a full-paying customer, and all these chocolates and goodies were totally undeserved. There was something painfully sham about it all. Every time I stepped into that private little mansion and saw yet another bowl of strawberries on the elegant glass-topped table, I winced. *Not again!*

When I finally went to check out, all the hotel clerks bowed and scraped. "How was your stay, Mr. Smith? Was everything all right?"

I put on a cheery smile. "Wonderful! I think I'll just move up here. Fantastic! Unbridled bliss!" I know something about diplomacy. But in my heart I whispered to myself that I just wanted to go home. At least there I pay the mortgage. I deserve my house.

Both stories point out humanity's deep reluctance to accept heaven's grace . . . and our insistence that somehow, someway, we can earn our own way to salvation. Even if all we have is a share of Isaiah's filthy rags (Isa. 64:6), we'll pile up enough of them to pay our own hotel bill. "Lord, those are Your three dollars. Now keep them! I'll scrape up my own somewhere."

As I mentioned in the introduction, I received an invitation to spend a week with the young adults at the Wisconsin Adventist camp meeting. Ten sermon slots! (I confessed to them on the first evening that in 10 sermons I could not only exhaust all my ideas on being good for a good reason—I could tell them everything I ever knew about *anything.* "By next Thursday we may even get into the quadratic formula and *Brady Bunch* trivia questions," I announced. It surprised me that attendance held up as well as it did.)

The bottom line, I suggested, was this: In 10 sessions I hoped to describe for them nine wonderful things "being good" would do for them . . . and one thing it *wouldn't.* And the one thing it wouldn't do forms our opening chapter.

Before getting on the plane, I had compiled a surprisingly long list of Bible texts that talk about obedience. Scripture offers *huge* reasons to obey. The Bible contains countless admonitions to follow the example of Christ, to glorify God in our lives, and to obey and observe the Decalogue. It upholds the saints of the last days as those who keep the commandments and have the faith of Jesus (Rev. 14:12). "By their fruits you will know them," Matthew 7:20, NKJV, declares. "Faith without works is dead," the apostle James reminds us (see James 2:17). And so on.

But the one thing obedience can't do is save us. That's the one no in a book of fascinating and, I hope, helpful yeses. While there are plenty of reasons to be good, earning a ticket to heaven just doesn't happen to be one of them. For some strange and wonderful reason heaven seems to be on a different currency system.

Back in 1992 my daughter Kami and I went to England for a 10-day trip. We had a great time, although some of the cooking was a bit skimpy. I joked to a friend afterward that I lost five pounds eating and she lost 200 pounds shopping. (Get it?)

The merchants there—and Kami made a point of befriending virtually every one of them in the whole British isles—were most happy to take her pound notes. Some of them even accepted dollar bills and graciously calculated the exchange rate for her so she wouldn't have to bother her pretty little head about it.

But I try to imagine the chaos if we had offered the clerk at Harrod's some Monopoly money. (And boy, I was tempted when I saw the prices there.) "Begging your pardon, sir, but we simply cannot accept these bills. They're not good here."

"But this is all I've got. I brought them all the way from California."

"I'm most dreadfully sorry . . ."

What a blow to discover that even my pile of orange 500s are out of favor!

My uncle, Morris Venden, likes to pose the question: "What if we get to heaven and discover that H.M.S. Richards, Sr., is not there? And in the mansion that had been prepared for him, we discover Adolf Hitler in residence instead?"

What?

Venden assures his congregations that he doesn't expect the above scenario to come to pass. However, "some we expect will not be there; others we *didn't* expect will be. There will be surprises."

Why? He concludes that it's hard for us to accept that *heaven is on the gift system all the way. Salvation is a gift.* Because of Calvary, heaven has adopted a different kind of currency. The suites there have indeed been paid for by Another. Our money is no good at the front desk.

"For by grace are ye saved through faith; and that not of yourselves: it is the gift of God: **Not of works, lest any man should boast**" (Eph. 2:8, 9).

Most world religions reject the concept of grace. I spent years as a missionary kid in Thailand watching the saffron-robed Buddhist priests going from house to house in the early morning Bangkok sun. Every family, no matter how poverty-ridden, would come to the front door with a small scoop of rice to give them.

Why? *Merit.* Every dab of rice given away was a point earned toward Nirvana, eternal bliss. The gods were surely watching.

These same people would gladly spend two baht (10 cents) at the Sunday market to buy a tiny sparrow in a cage. Having made their purchase, they would open the little bamboo gate and set the bird free. (What a racket for the entrepreneurs!) Again, a recorder of righteous deeds somewhere out there would take note of their small act of kindness.

And it is comforting to believe that way. Set a bird free, give away some rice, keep a few commandments, jog three miles a day, no smoke, no Coke. The strong among us much prefer a religion in which obedience is the qualifying ingredient. After all, they're good at practicing it.

In his book *Here I Come, Ready or Not*, Venden quotes from Arthur Spalding, who writes: "Most professed Christians believe that man must strive to be good and to do good, and that when he has done all he can, Christ will come to his aid and help him do the rest. In this confused credo of salvation partly by works and partly with auxiliary power, many trust today" (p. 38).

And Venden, whose book deals with last-day events and the great themes of Revelation and the three angels' messages, concludes: "This *subsidy religion* is Babylon" (p. 39).

Believe me, I quoted these comments at camp meeting knowing full well how easy it is to go down the other road and latch on to "cheap grace." To accept today's much-maligned "sin-and-live" theology casually. I hope the following nine chapters will tell a compelling story of the fruits of obedience. Grace certainly is *not* cheap. But I am glad that it is free.

Of course, the heart of the great Adventist righteousness-by-faith message is that a daily personal relationship with Christ is the essence of faith—with obedience springing naturally from that friendship. This makes all the more pointed Venden's observation: "When the majority of church members are finding no time, day by day, to spend seeking Jesus and His salvation, they are trying to save themselves, regardless of the words they speak" (*ibid.*, p. 37). No matter what our testimony regarding holy living—if we're not in a devotional relationship with Jesus, it's Babel and Babylon all over again. We are building our own pathetic little tower into the skies.

You know, I can say it and read it and believe it and even try to write a book about it. But it is devilishly easy to slip into counting up my acts of obedience and estimating their worth. *Let's see, I've got about 40 of these orange Monopoly bills now. Wow! Let's go shopping!* It's tough to believe and remember grace.

I heard of an Adventist pastor who sat down at a conference workers' meeting, only to discover that the topic was going to be righteousness by faith. "Again?" he asked. "We've heard that! Can't we go on to something else?"

That is a chilling response. Heaven cannot help us if we ever decide to indeed go on to something else. That "something else" is the enemy's agenda.

Yes, grace is beautifully followed by obedience—and I invite you again to stay tuned for some more chapters in this book. But I'm more thankful for grace. Recently I did a series of Voice of Prophecy scripts suggesting that the beloved hymn should not be "Amazing Grace." It should be "*More* Than Amazing Grace." Little things such as Kirk Gibson's 1988 World Series homer and cancer cures and *National Enquirer* headlines are amazing. But heaven's gift of grace is *more than* amazing.

I witnessed the power of that discovery from a most unlikely source: the NBC series finale of *L.A. Law*.

For eight years Arnie Becker, secular-minded divorce lawyer for McKenzie, Brackman, had terrorized the female population of southern California with his blatant womanizing. His mind-set was one of love 'em and leave 'em. Every now and then the empty ache of such night prowling would show through, but the following week Arnie would be on the make once again.

During the 1993-1994 season the show's writers introduced a new character: Jane Halliday. A born-again evangelical Christian, she permeated the law offices with her spirituality and occasional sermonizing.

Although I had tired of the program's silliness and steady cynicism, I began to watch with renewed interest. Especially with Arnie's lust radar honed in on this beautiful blond believer. Would Jane withstand his slick moves, his Bible quotations, his pretenses of spiritual interest?

On the last program Leland McKenzie, senior partner in the firm, announces that he has terminal cancer. The firm is breaking up. And fortysomething Arnold Becker begins to examine his barren soul for eternal answers.

For the first time the flirting over drinks and the one-night stands don't bring him satisfaction. Arnie is mortal . . . and he feels his mortality with a fresh anguish.

In a candid moment he pours out his fears to Jane. "Is this it? Is this all there is? In another 23 years I'm going to be McKenzie's age. That's no time at all. Your entire life happens in the wink of an eye. On the other hand, when you're dead, that's it. You're dead."

Jane looks at him. "There are those of us who believe otherwise."

"Do you believe otherwise?"

"Yes."

"So what do you do?"

She smiles. "I go to church."

He considers this, still feeling the twitch of male sensuality along with his curiosity. "Do you think that I might tag along with you sometime so that I might receive some of that same comfort?"

A nod. "I'm going tomorrow night. You're more than welcome."

Later in the episode Arnie is indeed at church . . . but sitting on the steps outside as choir music continues off-screen. Jane walks down the steps and sits down next to him. He still looks tormented.

"You all right?" she asks.

"Scared."

"What are you scared of?"

He gets right to it. "Dying."

Jane sighs. "I guess going to church didn't help."

Then Arnold Becker takes a deep breath and looks directly at her. "Jane, for the first time since I've known you, I want to be perfectly truthful. My interest in coming to church, just like my interest in reading the Bible . . . was just a means to an end. My real interest has always been getting you in the sack." (Please forgive the inclusion of this straightforward dialogue from the show transcript.)

Jane, who knew all this months ago, gives him a tiny smile of nonresentment. "Really?"

Arnie continues. "No, but I was sitting in there just now and I realized I shouldn't be pretending when it comes to things like this."

She thinks about this. "No, you probably shouldn't be." (Now listen to this.) "On the other hand, Jesus doesn't need for your heart to be pure in order for you to take comfort from Him."

The gospel of grace—preached on NBC's prime time Thursday night schedule. "Come to Jesus just as you are." But Arnold Becker doesn't believe it!

Shaking his head in despair, he cries out in protest. "You're not allowed to do that, Jane! Not allowed to lead this miserable life and then start asking for comfort just because you're terrified."

And then, in one of the great moments in this or any other television season, Jane looks at him and says: "Yes, you are."

Fade to black.

Even now I don't know if *L.A. Law*'s writers realized what they had stumbled onto that day. *Grace!* "'Yes, you are.' You're allowed to grab hold of it right now. Heaven's free gift is meant for all the Arnold Beckers of life. Including you."

I sat there watching with tears of wonderment in my eyes. For years I've tried to write grace-filled scripts for *It Is Written* and *The Voice of Prophecy,* only to have NBC come along and expose tens of millions of viewers to the gospel in one prime-time hour. Aren't God's providences incredible?

Ironically, this final episode about cancer and grace aired on the very same evening that Jackie Kennedy Onassis died of cancer. At the Voice of Prophecy we aired a special Sunday program the next week entitled *Jackie's Farewell: The Gospel and Arnie Becker*. It was too poignant an opportunity to pass up.

VOP speaker Lonnie Melashenko concluded at the end of that program: "*L.A. Law* called it quits last Thursday evening, so we'll never know if Arnold Becker accepted God's offer of grace. But you can, right now."

What wonderful news for Arnie—that an entire lifetime of selfish adultery and greed can be wiped away. That salvation has already been paid for. That his impure heart and lack of goodness and obedience need not be the determining factors in being accepted by a loving Jesus.

It's been suggested that Satan pours his greatest efforts into getting us to forget all about grace. To get us to work ourselves into a lather of false obedience—or give up in despair. To get us to cry out with Arnie: "You're not allowed to do that! 'Come to Jesus just as you are'? It's too good to be true."

But the good news *is* true. Our obedience is good for many things, but salvation is handled another way. Another kind of currency bearing the markings of Calvary has already paid the price.

What, then, is the role of obedience? If Arnie had accepted the good news that night on the church steps, would it have required a lifestyle change for him beginning at that point?

That is yet to come. And it will be seen that what follows is good news as well.

CHAPTER TWO

Picking Up My Socks

I asked the men at our Wisconsin camp meeting to raise their hands if they were married. About half of them were.

Then I instructed them, on the count of three, to call out their wife's worst fault. Well, I heard some nervous laughter—and they wouldn't do it. You would think I'd asked them to betray military secrets or something really big.

Art Buchwald, the syndicated humor columnist, once wrote an insightful piece entitled "Why Japanese Men Are Happy." It was an eye-opener to me as he described how a Japanese wife is still a slave to her husband and considers him to be "her only master on earth."

Now, much may have changed in the 30 years since he wrote this, but Buchwald paints a glowing picture of a Japanese wife who will go so far as to prostrate herself on the floor on her husband's side of the bed in the morning so that he won't have to step down on the cold floor. "It's small gestures like this that make for a solid marriage and a happy home," he observes.

He continues by telling how such a super wife stays home all day heating her husband's bathwater so it will be exactly the right temperature when he arrives home after a hard day at the office. She bows to him, helps him off with his clothes, washes him, dries him off, and will even give him a massage.

Isn't that marvelous stuff? I was impressed as I read it.

He concludes: "American women are afraid that if they offer to bathe their husbands, they will be considered inferior. This is ridiculous. A wife who knows how to bathe her husband in the Japanese style is a superior person and one whom any husband would be proud of stepping on when he gets out of bed in the morning."

I went to visit Wisconsin on a search for the *good* reasons to be good. And Art Buchwald has, in his own insightful way, brought us to one of the best. **Being good nurtures a relationship.**

The apostle Paul, in his letter to the Romans, describes a good kind of obedience, an "obedience that comes from faith" (Rom. 1:5, NIV). There is a goodness that is right, it seems, if it is a goodness, an obedience, that springs from a desire to deepen a friendship.

I'll admit that Buchwald and I have our tongues in cheek firmly in place when we gush on about wifely subservience and lying down on the cold floor for a mate. But is there a kind of marital goodness born out of a desire to make love grow?

In the seminar that I often present at churches, "Positive Parenting: A Christian Perspective," much of the curriculum focuses on marriage *behaviors*. Why? Is that legalism?

Consider, for example, romantic episodes. These moments of special joy take hard work and planning. Do such good deeds earn credit . . . or simply deepen our love?

Once when Lisa and I headed to Santa Barbara to visit some friends of ours, she was driving—and promptly proceeded to get us lost. I must confess that I was somewhat less than gracious about that.

Pulling off the road, she muttered glumly about running into a nearby hotel lobby to ask directions. I remained in the car, continuing to complain to myself about female intuition and map-reading skills.

A few moments later she emerged from the lobby and poked her head in the window. "Get out of the car—we're staying here tonight."

Blank stare. "Say what? Come on, we're late. Did they tell you where to go?"

"No, get out of the car. This is where we're staying."

I began to flush red. What was the matter with women anyway?

"What are you talking about? We're supposed to meet the Bishops at 4:00."

"No, we aren't. We're staying here, just you and me."

"I . . ."

As it turned out, the whole business of getting lost was a big fake. In fact, the plan to see the Bishops was itself a ruse. We were indeed staying at that lovely ocean-view hotel that evening. She had set up the whole thing, including lining up overnight baby-sitting for the kids. In the trunk of the car were toothbrushes, extra clothes, candlelight, and perfume—the works.

Now, the details of that evening are none of your business. Suffice it to say, it was a time of happy fellowship that only took place because somebody involved herself in a whole lot of works. The good deeds and obedience that lead to deepened love.

Now, is that legalism? Is it dead obedience to try to get the victory over nagging a spouse? I like to quote Ben Franklin: "Keep your eyes wide open before marriage . . . and half-shut afterward." Sometimes I have to grit my teeth to stay off certain topics. Why? Because I love my wife. Is effort like this good or isn't it?

Most couples have discarded that old-fashioned phrase in the marriage vows: "Love, honor, and *obey*." But 15 years of marriage have taught me that there is a right kind of obedience to the wants and needs of a spouse—a loving service that desires to bring us ever closer to each other.

I have often shared with others the personal discovery that has led to harmony in my relationship with Lisa. "Two simple steps," I tell people. "Number one, let her think she's getting her own way."

"What's number two?" someone always asks.

"Let her get her own way."

Well, OK, it's at best only a B-plus joke. But we sing "Have Thine own way, Lord," don't we? That involves obedience . . . hopefully because we really *do* want Him to have His own way in our lives. We love Him and want to be close to Him.

So I pick up my socks. I make the bed every morning. I mow the lawn for her every week. And it's gotten to where I like doing it. (I really do. Lisa's not making me write this part. There are a few other things she did order me to take out, but she's away at work at this moment.)

About a year ago I got a bright idea one Friday afternoon while mowing the lawn. (Hot sun beating down on my head, I guess.) Carefully I carved out an area of long grass that spelled out her name in huge letters. So we had a beautifully immaculate lawn with a big L-I-S-A right in the middle of it.

She came home that evening and didn't notice at first. Then while she was making supper she peeked out the window and saw the bedraggled grass still out there. Grumbling a little bit about my work, she went out to see why I'd missed so many spots. All of a sudden she saw what it said.

Let me just say that I could do no wrong for about a month after that. That LISA in the grass paid off for me like crazy. We had ice cream almost every night. In fact, she got up in Sabbath school a week later and told the entire church what a great husband she had. "David spelled my name in the lawn." She had it set to music and everything.

The next week I had about five phone calls from members wanting me to come and do their yards. "I don't mow lawns for a living," I protested the following Sabbath. "I have a nice job at the Adventist Media Center. And I'm really not a romantic. I just thought it was a great way to have less lawn to mow."

Even tiptoeing toward a new attitude regarding obedience can be a joyful experience. I think it is always rewarding to find that we can be involved in doing something for a bigger reason than we may have known was out there. Picking up my socks can have a kind of grandness if I see it as one puzzle piece in a vast and de-lightful 50-year marriage mosaic. And obedience to God's wishes takes on a special happiness when I sense that it is part of a deep, ever-enriching friendship.

But there is a flip side. Besides obedience there is *disobedience*. And at least in a marriage, disobedience—or, should we say, fla-grant disregard for the relationship—can be shattering. Leaving my socks on the floor every day for two weeks . . . sooner or later, it's going to do something to our relationship.

Let's explore this. What happens when I am careless and inattentive in treating my spouse well? Socks on the floor. Anniversaries ignored. Dodger ticket stubs from the past 15 seasons all over the bedroom dresser. Letting the backyard grow so high in weeds that Hollywood producers want to come and shoot Tarzan movies back there.

Let me propose to you that I have the perfect spouse—the forever-patient, long-suffering, always-forgiving Lisa. (This is very nearly true.) She has an Energizer heart that could overlook something 490 times and keep on loving. I might leave my socks on the floor until they begin coming out the chimney, and she'd keep on loving me with an enduring love.

However, a deadly truth eventually surfaces. If I keep on shrugging and dropping socks long enough, *I'm going to stop caring about her.* It has always worked that way, and it always will.

I might have a God whose patience is infinite. He might be willing to forgive me for the same stupid thing a million times. (Evidence suggests this.) But if in my life I continue over and over to disdain Him through careless, casual living and sinning, I can guarantee that the time will come when I simply stop caring about Him anymore. There really can be no such thing as sin-and-live.

On a purely human level, it's a fact that sin gets in the way of our friendships. Lying and meanness and gossip and unkind words and selfish attitudes shatter relationships all the time. Sin wrecks our connectedness with each other.

A number of years ago our family was on the way home after a week of vacation. Trying to drive 500 miles in an un-air-conditioned Datsun in August is not the best end to a holiday, but that was our Sunday objective.

Karli, who was probably 5 at the time, and perspiring freely in the back seat, is one of the best little travelers I know. Gracious and patient through thick and thin, cold or hot. But she was bored.

Now, virtually every 5-year-old in the country shares two interesting character traits. They love to sing or hum little kiddie tunes. Second, they are not in the least bit bothered if they don't happen to know all the words to something.

But you put those two characteristics together in a hot car, and bad things can happen.

We were still about 150 miles away when Karli began to sing that little song: "Mickey Mouse . . . Mickey Mouse." (I can't put notes in here, but you know the one.)

Unfortunately, that was all she knew. The rest of the words escaped her. But that did not bother Karli. "Mickey Mouse . . . Mickey Mouse . . . uh . . . Mickey Mickey Mickey Mickey Mouse." Then again: "Mickey Mouse . . . Mickey Mouse . . . ."

Well, she sang that identical refrain for probably a half hour. While her happiness heartened me for the first three or four minutes, there came a time when the repetition began to take on the aura of a Chinese water torture.

But she kept on bravely. "Mickey Mouse . . . Mickey Mouse . . ." My hands tightened on the steering wheel.

Finally I couldn't take it any longer. Clearing my throat, I gently said, "Honey, I'm so glad you're singing and are such a cheerful kid. It's wonderful. But please, no more songs about Mickey Mouse. OK?" *Keep it light.*

"OK."

A long pause. "Minnie Mouse. Minnie Mouse . . . Minnie Minnie Minnie . . ."

After about two minutes of this, the red light came on again. "Uh, honey?"

"What?"

"I, uh, I'm glad you're having fun and singing and everything like that. But no more songs about mice of any kind. Male or female. Please, no mice. OK?"

A long pause. "Plu-to. Plu-to. Ploo-hoo-hoo-hoo-hoo-hoo-hoo-hoo-hoo-hoo-to." (He's the dog in Disney cartoons.)

The Datsun swerved abruptly to the side of the road. "Get out and walk! It's about 85 miles—you can probably get home by Tuesday. Just take I-5 to 405 to 118 east. Lisa, give her a sandwich or something."

Do you see how even innocent *naughtiness* can drive people apart?

Let me be blunt in saying that some kinds of sin make it difficult to establish a relationship. Don't you find it hard to be best friends with someone whose heart is filled, for example, with racist thoughts or a natural meanness?

About a year ago I had the challenging experience of carpooling with a person who was from what I would call the "really Religious Right." He made Pat Robertson and Jerry Falwell sound like liberal subversive atheists. Night after night he would zoom down the freeway veering wildly from topic to topic in a display of exhausting free association, telling me why virtually everything in America from gun laws to supermarkets to taxes to cable television to Bambi should be abolished. I mean, he hated everything in the state of Georgia because that's where the Braves played and they were owned by Ted Turner, who was married to Jane Fonda, who was a Communist, and all her movies show what's wrong with Hollywood today and . . . and . . . and . . . I mean, he was against *everything*.

Although I tried to get to like him, all that venom created a 20-foot-high barrier between us. I just couldn't get past it. Was he serious that we should take over Canada by military force? (I agreed with him about the Braves, though.)

It is a good sign when we get to a point in our relationships, especially with God, when the greatest sin-ache has to do with the damage to that relationship.

Consider the story of King David's great fall. A woman was illicitly pregnant. A husband lay dead on the battlefield, betrayed by David's calculating desire to get something that was not his. Trusted associates had been trapped in the web of Bathsheba-gate.

All these elements brought despair to David when the truth came out. Which is good and proper. A man was dead and people had been hurt.

But King David's heartsickness came primarily from the fact that things were not right between him and God. Even more than forgiveness, he wanted the comfort of knowing that the relationship was back on track. "Do not cast me from your presence or take your Holy Spirit from me. Restore to me the joy of your salvation" (Ps. 51:11, 12, NIV). That is a good sorrow.

Just a few weeks ago I felt a bit of that same good sorrow. A valued friend and I had gotten into a fairly vicious argument at work. I had really ripped away at him in a public way that was not only unfair, but abruptly pulled into the open some views I'd been holding on to far too long.

We had a phone conversation that night that only made matters worse. For almost an hour I sat there in the living room, feeling the sickening deadness of estrangement. I was wrong, and I knew it—and the chasm was an ugly thing. It was literally a kind of physical hurt.

I had to leave at 3:30 the next morning for a flight across the country, so Lisa and I went to bed early. The minute I reached my hotel room in Dallas I dialed my friend, determined to make things right, only to find that he'd hiked over to my home the night before at 10:15, hoping to find a light on. He'd felt the same agony over the split and had longed to build a bridge too. What a beautiful guy! And what a flood of relief to know that the separations caused by sin *can* be swept away.

Growing in Jesus is a slow process—"the work of a lifetime"—but I begin to sense the first glimpses of excitement brought by obeying God for the sheer pleasure of pleasing Him. Spending time in prayer and realizing that He appreciates the time too. Singing praise music in church as a tangible way of letting Him know I honestly do think He is "an awesome God."

As with any friendship, I have to go through the hard times, the dry spells. Occasions when obedience isn't fun, when the Bible is dull. Our time together is listless, maybe for days on end. But that's even true of a marriage! We "carry on" with our spouse, knowing that a mountaintop experience follows every spiritual valley.

Thank God, things don't come to an end when we sin—in our marriages or with Him, either! Ellen White kindly points out in *Steps to Christ:* "Even if we are overcome by the enemy, we are not cast off, not forsaken and rejected of God" (p. 64). Pick yourself up and carry on. All good relationships continue through the mistakes and shortcomings.

In parish after parish Morris Venden fixes his congregation with a pastoral gaze and quietly asks them, "Are you spending time alone with God every morning getting to know Him?" That is hard work, but happy obedience framed in friendship can happen no other way.

My wife and I resolved some years ago that 52 Sabbaths a year, if humanly possible, we would be sitting together in church. Now, travel for the Adventist Media Center takes me away for a number of weekends every year. But if I'm in town, we're in church. If we want to go to the beach or the mountains, we wait until the afternoon. If we're both out of town together, we find the nearest Adventist church and sit down in a pew there.

Is that kind of Sabbathkeeping legalism? A vain counting up of merit points? I don't believe it is, because we find that our time together on Sabbath mornings greatly nurtures our relationship with Christ.

I understand full well that I don't earn one thousandth of a ticket to heaven by observing the Sabbath or by going to church x weeks in a row. Salvation cannot be attained using that Monopoly currency. But those three hours at the Thousand Oaks Adventist Church are just about the biggest factor in our friendship growth with Christ. And friendship with Jesus seems to have a lot to do with salvation.

(Let me say right here that there are more important things in this universe even than whether I am saved or not. Keep reading.)

What, then, is our focus? Do we *gaze* at the law and tote up the Sabbaths in church? Well, we gaze a little bit . . . just to make sure the relationship isn't drifting away. With Lisa, I do think about the socks and the backyard once in a while. But we pour our main energy into the friendship. We focus on the friendship.

As mentioned earlier, the enemy would like for us to forget about grace. He's equally pleased if we think endlessly about obedience without remembering the friendship. For me to have a consecutive-Sabbaths-at-church streak going like the Orioles' Cal Ripken is fine with him . . . especially if I've stopped tasting the goodness of a friendship with God during that streak.

It's said that Martin Luther once descended from the cathedral balcony where he had just delivered an exceptionally good sermon. And the first parishioner to greet him told him so in gushing terms.

"Outstanding, Brother Martin! Totally awesome! *Ausgezeichnet!*" Or words to that effect.

He held up a hand. "I know," he murmured. "The devil already told me that on my way down the steps."

I mentioned Philip Yancey's article "Why Be Good?" in the introduction. He describes a grief-laden experience with summer school where he had to learn German. Evening after grueling evening he hunched over a too-small desk as the instructor droned on about noun genders and grammar. Outside, his peers walked by the lake and flew kites.

And the rules! Homework and extra reading and sheets to fill out and an instructor to pay attention to. Obedience was a wretched, wearying experience.

Then one day he met Inga. Beautiful, charming, lovely. He had a great interest in getting to know her better. In fact, he was head over heels in love.

But she spoke only German. Not a word of English.

I'll bet you can guess what happened next.

CHAPTER THREE

The Ballad of Chelsea and Socks

I hope the following story is apocryphal, but I have no way of knowing.

A man on an airplane had clearly had far too much to drink. As it appeared to those nearby, he must have boarded the plane half loaded and proceeded from there. He smelled like a distillery. His loud, slurred comments about the airline food, the flight attendants' anatomies, and the world in general were offensive in the extreme. His reddened eyes, rumpled and beer-stained clothes, and boozy odor hinted that it was a regular way of life for the man in seat 19C.

Finally one of the flight attendants decided to confront him. Leaning gingerly into the alcoholic haze that surrounded the passenger, she whispered in an insistent voice, "Shhh! Please try to be quiet, sir. Don't you know that the Reverend Billy Graham is sitting right behind you?"

What? The man sat upright in befuddled delight. "Grilly Baham? I mean, Billy Graham? I *love* Billy Graham!"

He struggled to turn around in his seat, fumbling with numbed fingers to undo his seat belt. Finally he was able to pull himself to a kneeling position and look around at the row of passengers behind him. Sure enough, there sat Billy Graham with his Bible, a determinedly passive expression on his face.

"Billy Graham?" the drunk roared happily, his voice echoing up and down the entire plane.

"Yes." That soft, pastoral Southern Baptist voice loved by millions.

The volume went up a notch as the man's bulky frame swayed precariously. "I want you to know, Mishter Graham . . . what a . . . what a . . . what a *differensh* you've made in my life!"

How do you respond to a testimonial like that? I've wondered how many moms have listened to sons stand before a crowd and proclaim "Everything I am today I owe to my mother" and thought to themselves, *Did you have to say that?*

Lately Lisa and I have found ourselves often quoting—and thinking about—a new favorite verse. "Let your light so shine before men that they may see your good works **and glorify your Father which is in heaven**" (Matt. 5:16).

Somehow that one verse seems to set right a major part of this discussion about being good. Why do it? As a means of giving glory to God! I want my life indelibly and publicly stamped with the tag "Christian" to make God look good.

Adventists equally love a companion verse: "So whether you eat or drink or whatever you do, do it all for the glory of God" (1 Cor. 10:31, NIV). To honor God is an excellent motivation for obedience—in fact, it's the best one.

It is an awesome thing to bear the name of someone you love and admire. I am, and will be through eternity, a Smith. Of course, that's the biggest club in the world, but I'm the son of D. Kenneth Smith.

That's different.

And I want to live in a way that will honor *that* Smith.

Back in the sorry spring of 1974 I found myself suspended from college for a quarter. My parents, still serving a mission term in Bangkok, didn't get the news for a week or two. When they finally heard about it, my dad wept.

Those tears caused me more anguish than I can ever describe to you. I had failed him. For months I had walked the sidewalks of that college campus with the name of Smith. It was printed in 2,000 yearbooks scattered across the nation. And as a Smith I had been kicked out of school.

I don't ever want to hurt my dad that way again. And you can believe that my love for him has an impact on my behavior. I *want* to obey because of Dad.

I'll never forget the first time I watched my fiancée sign her name "Lisa Jean *Smith*." Wow! The wedding was still a month away, but we were filling out banking papers, and she would soon be a Smith. Lisa Jean *Smith*. A smile passed between us—we knew it was a special moment.

And for 16 years she has been a marvelous Smith. There has been a bit of Matthew 5:16 even in our marriage relationship.

So we are Smiths. But I'm also part of the Venden clan—and my three brothers and seven cousins and I know what that means.

And I carry the name of Christian. If you're reading this, you probably do too. It's wonderful—and a bit frightening, isn't it?

(The thought just flashed into my mind that we immediately experience a bit of *unity* there, don't we? A common loyalty to that name. More later.)

To be the child of the president of the United States has got to be a scary thing, as I'm sure Chelsea Clinton and others have discovered. Everything you say and do reflects on your father's entire administration. Even Socks the cat was expected to be a good example.

Everybody in the world hears about it when somebody named Reagan appears in a nude pictorial in *Playboy* magazine or does that infamous *Saturday Night Live* gig dressed only in a nice shirt and Presidential underwear. For four years a good ol' Georgia boy named Billy made headlines with every beer and belch.

In a way, you've got to feel sorry for them. A teenage girl named Susan (Ford) never went out on a date without two Secret Service men tagging along. When she finally married, comedian Bob Hope cracked that the wedding march should be replaced by "Me and My Shadow."

All those who bear the name—or align themselves with a movement—are, like it or not, participants in the reputation of that movement. It's a common fact that there are only about four Democrats at the Adventist Media Center. One hundred forty-six

Republicans and four Democrats. The Dems hold their monthly rallies in one of the VOP's broom closets.

Naturally, I'm not about to give away which side I'm on, but I will admit that every time someone hears a good Clinton joke or sees a new cartoon making fun of the president, they send it to my desk by interoffice mail. (Lately seven or eight times a week. I had to add a second secretary just to open the mail.) Coupons for 50 cents off a $200 haircut—things like that.

Which is fine! For 12 years I dished it out. Now I can take it. Let me say it again: when we are part of a movement, we participate in the public's perception of that movement.

This is why the televangelist scandals of recent years were agony for the body of Christ. The brush of a few public sins tarred all of Christianity. It's painfully true that Matthew 5:16 cuts both ways. All that hypocrisy and covering up and tear-stained "confessions" on TV penalized the whole Christian church back to the two-yard line, so to speak. You can believe we felt its impact at the Adventist Media Center.

You can see why any thought of exploiting "cheap grace" is unthinkable for the Christian. Sin and live? A Florida motel room party on Saturday night followed by a coast-to-coast televised church service the next morning? It is simply not possible for the Christian because of Matthew 5:16. We don't dare hurt our Lord's reputation that way.

Of course, it goes deeper than just the risk of getting caught when Miss Hahn tells all. The late Richard Nies, in his book *The Security of Salvation*, describes his relationship with his own family. They loved him, he wrote in amazement, even when he did unloving things. Did that give him freedom to carouse and live in adultery and sin freely? Did their attitudes of grace and promises of forgiveness open the floodgates to sin?

"On the contrary," he writes, "it is the reason I would be *ashamed* to do so. Because they are what they are, because they do love me in spite of myself when I do things that are wrong, I feel ashamed. Rather than opening up the floodgates to sin, it is as we see and fully understand God's love for us that the floodgates of sin close" (pp. 27, 28).

Why Be Good?

God takes a great risk when He lets us carry His name. I'm awed that He allows me to be a Christian. I mean, everybody's watching! And people will make up their minds about God based on what they see in me. It takes my breath away even to consider it.

It's a very fair and reasonable disclaimer, then, that John makes to the believers. "No one who lives in him keeps on sinning. No one who continues to sin has either seen him or known him" (1 John 3:6, NIV). A man or woman living a life of willful disdain for God's law, of *continual* disobedience, shouldn't keep carrying the banner. After all, everybody's watching.

Moses, probably more than any other living human, understood the value of God's reputation. It was a noble moment in biblical history when he said to the Lord, "If You can't forgive these people without forever tarnishing Your own image . . . then blot my name out too." Moses would rather be lost than have any part in diminishing God's reputation in the earth.

I think we've all been raised to believe that there is nothing more important than our salvation. But there is! God's reputation is more crucial even than my getting into heaven. God's victory over evil is a greater issue than whether or not I have a mansion in His kingdom.

Hopefully I can help God's reputation by *being* saved. But as I read Matthew 5:16 and consider that Moses was willing to sacrifice his own eternity for the sake of God's good name among the nations, I start to sense that you and I are players in something that is wonderfully big.

We are being good for a cause that is larger than perhaps we ever dreamed. Our obedience, lovingly offered in order to honor God and elevate Him up before a watching universe, is grander, braver, more visionary than words can describe. We are playing our part in a great movement that has a glorious climax ahead if we stay the course.

I said to my Wisconsin friends, "You don't win any carnival coupons for obeying the seventh commandment. We don't earn salvation by hanging in there in our marriages for 50 or 60 years." And of course, camp meeting is a time when you see all the dear little old couples walking around. Still holding hands after all these decades, carrying their folding chairs over to the big tent. Little shriveled men with their polyester pants pulled up almost to their neck, still taking their wives' arms and leading them to a comfortable spot in the shade before the afternoon sermon.

Praise God for them! They haven't earned salvation by their faithful golden anniversary marriages . . . but they sure do make God look good. That kind of marital loyalty marvelously testifies to the power of Jesus in their lives. Don't you agree? You don't find too many couples *out there* who hang in for 60 years, but those little Adventist mom-and-pop teams are doing it. Fantastic!

And all those loyal Sabbathkeepers in Wisconsin don't win a heavenly home by their obedience. But they honor God when, week by week, their neighbors see the car pull out of the garage and head off to church. "There goes that Adventist family," they muse to themselves. "All dressed up every Saturday. And they always wave to us, real friendly-like. Plus they keep bringing us cupcakes. Hmmm." And God's reputation goes up a notch.

I mentioned in the book *Heaven* my experience of playing in a Christian softball league in Arroyo Grande. On opening day I foolishly suggested that all losers should be required to join the denomination of the league champions. Fortunately, everybody voted my proposal down—otherwise I'd be a member of the Foursquare Church now.

The team with the biggest built-in advantage seemed to be the Assembly of God squad. When one of their players was hurt on a play, they would simply lay hands on him and the injury was immediately healed. Down by six runs? They'd go off to a corner of the dugout and pray in tongues . . . and emerge to score 10.

But the most memorable experience I had was against the players from Calvary Church. The first season they were in the league they were the biggest screamers you ever saw. They whined on every play. "Come on, ump, that guy's using a spitball." (It was slow pitch.) I mean, they were an embarrassment.

One year later something had happened to them. Somehow, during the off-season, these guys had decided that they would honor God during every game. "Matthew 5:16" became their new club motto.

You could hardly believe the change. They were kind and gracious *on every play*. If they struck out, that was fine. Dropped a pop fly? Fine. Losing a tough one in the bottom of the last inning when their right fielder let one go through his legs to the wall? They'd trot right in and begin shaking the opposing team's hands. "Great game, you guys! Far out! Praise the Lord! Can you stick around for some doughnuts?"

Don't get me wrong. They still played hard. They were intense, good players who knew the game. In fact, that's part of what made their witness so effective. Winning most of the time, they completely shattered the myth that Christian players play a lackadaisical game and then shrug when they lose. "Hey, man . . . God's will." But they had become the most Christian athletes I had ever encountered. We saw their good works, and you'd better believe they made sure we gave the honor to their Father who is in heaven.

Maybe they'd been reading the book of Daniel, where excellence of performance provided Daniel and his friends constant opportunities to reflect well on their God. Three different times Nebuchadnezzar and then Darius whistled for the crowd's attention and declared, "The God these men serve . . . apparently He's the one."

Note that it is the excellence of performance, the *obedience,* that earns one the right to give God honor. I was in Dodger Stadium in 1988 the night that Orel Hershiser beat the New York Mets 6-0 in game 7 of the NL play-offs to take L.A. into the World Series.

Baseball fans will remember that Hershiser had just concluded one of the most amazing feats in baseball: surpassing Don Drysdale's consecutive-inning scoreless streak. For nearly 60 innings in a row he'd shut down the opposition.

He was also a born-again Christian, as the watching world well knew. Now as 60,000 fans stood on their feet counting down the last three outs and cheering every pitch, he disposed of Howard Johnson, the last Met batter.

"Strike three called!" And with hundreds of millions of people observing via satellite around the globe, Hershiser stepped off the mound and then knelt down in a moment of prayer. The celebration on the field paused for just a few glorious seconds as this Christian athlete gave credit to God for the excellence of his season. My brother and I both had tears in our eyes.

The diligence, the hard work, the obedience earned him that incredible media opportunity. His life that October spelled out "Matthew 5:16" before an audience we could never measure.

But in your own small way you are privileged to do the same. We are all Daniels. People are watching. More often than we know, we have the chance to make our God look good.

I find it exciting that the principle found in Matthew also applies to the church. The reputation of Christianity, and especially of the Adventist faith, rests upon the performance of its adherents. We might wish it to be otherwise, but facts are facts. People will decide about the church based on what they see in us.

There's an expression in public relations that PR hacks like me have sometimes wished we had the guts to say to the boss: "I can't *say* good until you *do* good." No sense in broadcasting "an exciting new breakthrough" if the product stinks.

We want to be called the caring church. Well, then, what are the facts of the matter? Specifically, what does your life and demeanor do to support the validity of that slogan? Is your Adventist church family really "the caring church"—and especially made so because you're there each week?

When you dine out with your non-Adventist coworkers at a restaurant to celebrate someone's birthday, does your vegetarianism wear a gracious and cheerful face? Or does the way you handle something like that needlessly make you the company geek?

I don't want to go down a long list of similar questions, hurting a lot of feelings (especially my own). But lately I have sensed what a marvelous opportunity we have to make the Adventist message seem either winsome . . . or strange.

And I'm deeply grateful for people among us who live out Matthew 5:16 with almost effortless brilliance. I was teaching a mathematics class in a public college one evening. During the break one young woman approached me. "Tell me, Mr. Smith," she began.

"Yes?"

"Why is it that Adventists are always so . . ."

She knew about my church background, obviously. But it makes the hair stand up on the back of your neck when a sentence begins like that. I braced myself.

"Why are Adventists always so . . . cheerful and kind?"

Yes! Yes! Yes! Somewhere out there are some wonderfully cool Adventist Christians who had made her sit up and take note. Praise God for them, wherever they are. I hope to be counted among their number.

Let me say it again: we're into something big here. Obedience becomes almost an exhilarating experience when it's part of such a breathtaking campaign.

It makes being good kind of fun.

CHAPTER FOUR

Too Many John Wayne Movies

A number of years ago someone conducted an interesting study of men going into a theater to watch a John Wayne film. Clandestine cameras and all that.

As they walked into the theater their behavior was normal. But something fascinating happened to virtually every male as he came out of the theater. Can you guess?

That's right. Or I should probably say "Yep." There was an unmistakable swagger to the step of almost every man in the crowd. After two hours of watching John Wayne on the silver screen, it was easy to see the difference in how men walked as they strutted to their cars.

I never heard if the people recording the theater patrons interviewed any of the men to see if they had detected this subliminal change in themselves. I can just imagine how it would go: "Wa-al, now, little lady, ah never thought o' that. Walkin' funny? Shoot, ah walk just like ah always have. Get along now, ya hear? Ah got to go round up mah dogies." Right.

It's hard to imagine grown men being so easily swayed by a John Wayne film. Now me—ah'm totally impervious to the Wayne persona. It don't impact me none. No way, mister.

What once did get to me was the debonair way Agent 86 would go down all those corridors during *Get Smart*. So suave. Max had that cocky little way about him as he would pass through those doors that silently slid open for him. Then the way he would go into that phone booth, dial the number, and then duck out of sight. What a guy!

Sometimes I would find myself walking down a hallway at school, imitating that smooth walk and humming the theme music from the show. "Sorry about that, 99—I can't kiss you now. There are KAOS agents all over the place and my shoe phone is busted." *Oh, Dave, you're so cool.*

It doesn't take a Week of Prayer to convince me that the Bible is speaking the truth when it says that we become changed by beholding. Day by day we all find ourselves being molded into the image of those things we most admire. "Beholding" does a number on a person. America is swamped right now with pint-sized Michael Jordan sports fans who want nothing more than to "be like Mike."

And so this leads to yet another reason to be good:

Christians have a burning desire to copy Jesus in everything they do. We'll naturally be good if we are hanging around the One who most embodies goodness.

It's such a shallow cliché: "Imitation is the sincerest form of flattery." We've learned to speak almost scornfully of a person telling a boss, "Great tie, J.R.! Where can I get one just like it?" And yet Christians need to be reminded that copying the life and tactics and character of Jesus Christ, when motivated by love and admiration, is the best kind of obedience there is.

John the beloved disciple is a remarkable example of this. He underwent a three-and-a-half-year transformation that took him from being a "son of thunder" who voted for fire to come down on his enemies to the one who said, "Beloved, let us love one another." Nothing could effect that kind of change in a person except to spend quality time with the Prince of Peace. Though unaware of it in himself, his friends surely noticed the miraculous results.

For good or for ill, your friend David B. Smith is as susceptible as anyone to the kind of character molding that comes from beholding. Several years ago I worked with a good friend for a number of months on a film screenplay. We'd spend hours together at a time scrapping over dialogue and certain scenes.

Too Many John Wayne Movies

Now, Wayne is a great guy, courteous and hardworking, a genuinely good person. But his religious philosophy is very different from mine. There's nothing sinister about it, just a case of two people coming into adulthood from different backgrounds.

It happens that his vocabulary contains what is probably the average amount of "saltiness" for a typical nonbeliever. Low-to-medium. And as we spent long hours together in writing and storyboarding sessions at his house, I began to notice just the slightest bit of an edge creeping into my own expressions. Now, my words were certainly milder than his. But I could not deny that a change had occurred. When you swim in the ocean, you're going to get some salt on you and in you.

How, then, does the Christian combat this tendency to be stained by beholding the corrupt world that swirls around us?

Of course, we respond with the obvious: *Stay away from the bad and immerse yourself with the good.* Don't spend so much time at Wayne's house—go to prayer meeting instead. Hang around with Spirit-filled men and women.

When I go on a trip with my boss, Pastor Lonnie Melashenko, who is speaker of the Voice of Prophecy, I find my conversations and thoughts uplifted. We pray a lot. Discussions seem to focus on spiritual goals, on reaching people for Jesus. Same thing with Mark Finley, whom I've worked with for years at It Is Written. Something wonderful happens to you when you hang around with Mark. He is one spiritual man!

Hanging around with Christ will do the same for us. By beholding, we become changed—and so many of us simply are not looking at the right things.

One who knew has advised us that it is good to spend "a thoughtful hour" each day contemplating the life of Jesus. And yet the Christian community, including people who live on Seville Court in Newbury Park, California, is too content to settle for what Morris Venden describes as a Bible verse and a quick prayer—with our hand on the doorknob as we head out of the house in the morning. Some beholding!

It's become clear to me that real beholding and transforming will never take place until we become serious about focusing on Jesus as a tightly programmed *daily* habit. When we do really look at our number one Hero for substantial amounts of time each and every day—only then do things begin to happen.

I'm finding it to be good news that good habits can slowly become as strong as the bad habits used to be. Once I have firmly established and locked it in concrete *and* given it some time to build up its own scheduling "momentum," a daily encounter with Jesus starts to have some staying power.

(Lisa and I have found the real answer. Get up at a ghastly early hour of the morning and go running for five or six miles. After 50 minutes of that, sitting down for a quiet period of Bible study will seem like sheer joy in comparison. Try it! You'll soon be an on-fire skinny Christian.)

Much has been written about the successful devotional life and its transforming power. I'll settle for pointing you to the few pages in the well-loved classic *Patriarchs and Prophets* that deal with the life of Enoch. E. G. White says very simply: "Enoch reached a higher experience; he was drawn into a closer relationship with God" (p. 84). She then describes in brief detail how 300 years of incredible devotion made Enoch a man of singular witnessing power. Clearly he was changed more than other men and women—"communing thus with God, Enoch came more and more to reflect the divine image" (p. 87).

And of course we treasure the hints of that hidden moment, more mysterious and wonderful than human imagination, when Enoch suddenly vanished. How did it happen? No one knows. White observes quietly that "for three centuries he had walked with God. Day by day he had longed for a closer union; nearer and nearer had grown the communion, **until God took him to Himself.** He had stood at the threshold of the eternal world, only a step between him and the land of the blest; and now the portals opened, the walk with God, so long pursued on earth, continued, and he passed through the gates of the Holy City—the first from among men to enter there" (p. 87).

Here is the ideal heaven holds out for us: obedience that comes from an ever-intensifying fellowship with a Saviour who is good. An obeying that is fun, that is happily natural.

Not only do we find our lives transformed by such fellowship, but we also learn the life strategies that made Jesus' brief experience on earth such a success. How did He fight temptation? How did He accomplish so much so soon? Time spent with Him will give us the answers.

When Mark Finley and I worked together on the *Discover Jesus* book and television series back in 1992, we explored the secrets of Christ's success. The vital principle, of course, was that Jesus endeavored nothing in His own power. "By myself I can do nothing" (John 5:30, NIV). He took His every action in cooperation with God's will for His life. All day, every day, He placed Himself in the hands of His Father. "Not My will, but Thine be done."

And then Mark and I outlined four life principles that Jesus regularly practiced. **Prayer. Bible study. Fellowship with other Christians. Practical service for others.** They were the building blocks that helped Jesus fortify Himself to meet Satan's attacks, that gave Him answers when challenged by the Pharisees, that provided Him with power to work miracles, and that kept His focus on saving the world rather than Himself.

Let me say it again: If Jesus is our hero, then we *will* copy Him. We'll gladly adopt His blueprint. And obedience will become joy.

This miracle of transformation is, of course, translated down to the next generation—from Christians to those who watch Christians. Already we have mentioned the sobering fact that "everybody's watching," and it will come up again in subsequent chapters.

Surely it's fair to assume that if by beholding Christians are becoming changed, then people will draw conclusions about the character of Christ *by watching His followers*. Christ's followers validate the Christian life in the trenches. It's been suggested that we are the only "Jesus" many people will ever see.

So day by day you and I are participants in a kind of divine "transitive property." (That's the one that goes: If a = b and b = c, then a = c.) Which translates into the Christian realm as follows: "If

David S. is a certain way, and he is supposedly like Christ, then Christ is that certain way as well."

Those looking on may or may not grant allowances for my rate of growth in the Christian life. This can either terrify us or become a hope-filled and wonderful challenge. We can be living testaments.

In recent years, as I've worked on authoring the Bucky Stone teen adventure series, this idea of personal influence has found its way into the story lines. Bucky is a young person who has an extraordinary relationship with Jesus—and a personality that brings easy friendships. He wields more than his share of influence, both among his peers and within his own family.

Book 8, *Summer Camp Scars,* has a scene in which he is babysitting his 8-year-old sister, Rachel Marie. After an evening of riding bikes together and studying her primary Sabbath school lesson, he tucks her into bed. A quiet little bedside conversation ensues during which they talk about baptism. He ends up asking her why she wants to be baptized.

"I want to be like you, Bucky," she answers in a drowsy but admiring voice. And he's frozen by those words. A high school junior . . . and a young child's salvation very likely depends on his influence.

My friends who are Bucky Stone fans know that he lives up to the challenge. His secret is what ours must be: daily time in fellowship, in beholding, in gazing upon Jesus' face.

And Bucky can be tough in shouldering that responsibility. Later in the same book he faces down an older guy, one of the camp counselors that he's discovered down in the boat shed with a marijuana cigarette. And our young hero delivers a blistering lecture to the pot-smoking phony. "Man, you're God to these guys here!"

Is it wearying to always be an influence (undoubtedly the PK's greatest curse), to always be "on"? I may be tempted to wonder how Jesus felt in that regard until I remember that Jesus was so attuned to the Father's desires for Him that when obeying He was but following His own highest impulses anyway. He experienced obedience that was 100 percent natural.

This divine "transitive property" works in our social relationships as well. Getting A to equal C can also happen when we deliberately place our lives in contact with godly friends, with Spirit-filled men and women. Our characters are also transformed by being in their proximity, and if they are daily growing more like Jesus, we can, in a sense, be swept along with them.

One of my earliest memories as a little missionary child in Thailand was that of working for my Busy Bee pin. Now, I was only 3 years old at the time, but rules were lax out there 9 million miles from Pathfinder World Headquarters. The local club was desperate for recruits.

And here is how I succeeded: My dad would say to Dan, my older brother (age 5), "Show me five flowers." Dan would scurry around in our front yard and point to five different kinds.

"How about you, David?"

With a confident smile, I lisped, "The same ones Danny just showed you."

"Those are yours too?"

"Uh-huh."

At the age of 3 I was a bonafide Busy Bee graduate. I still remember walking up onto the church platform in my little short khaki pants (Dan claims my diaper was hanging out from the bottom, but I don't recall any such thing) to receive my pin. Dad and the local church elders solemnly shook my hand as I was duly honored.

Yep, it's all in who you hang around with! Grab yourself some smart, Bible-reading, Holy Spirit-transformed Christian friends, and just do what you see them doing. Within limits, of course, as you keep your eyes focused most of all on our supreme Example.

CHAPTER FIVE

Cleaning Out the Trunk of My Car

I'm going to make a confession now that will probably cause you to throw down my book with a grunt and mutter, "This guy's totally nuts." But I have to be honest, so here goes: *I ran the 1995 Los Angeles Marathon.*

It's not totally my fault. My wife has completed the race twice, and after a while the buildup of injured masculine pride just got to be too much. (Especially after all that John Wayne strutting around from the last chapter.)

So on March 5, 1995—one day after my fortieth birthday—I somehow staggered around the 26-mile track. [Editor's note: to protect David B. Smith's reputation, his time for the race will remain a secret.]

I was somewhat comforted by the knowledge that the L.A. race seems to attract fools anyway. Rock-and-roll bands play on every street corner as the runners lurch past. People run in 90-degree heat wearing gorilla outfits. Some push their grandmothers along in strollers. A few years ago a huge contingent of runners came as Elvis impersonators, complete with their white jumpsuits and pompadour wigs. (Incredibly, most of them finished.)

For a long time I pondered what strategy I would employ. At one point I leaned toward the Rosie Ruiz Plan, in which you take a taxi for the first 26 miles and then just run the last 385 yards, bursting across the finish line without a bead of perspiration anywhere on you. Lisa saw certain moral problems with that, but I felt that it was either that or dying at the age of 40 and one day.

Living so close to the marathon phenomenon for these past few years has given me at least a little bit of "insider" understanding. Have you noticed how all the runners have a sign on their shirt with a big number on it? And right below the number is some writing in small print? People watching on TV have always wondered what it says, and I can now reveal what's printed there: "I Am an Idiot."

But seriously, folks . . .

Preparing for the race I discovered that those who want to finish a marathon put away certain things if they want to win (*win* being translated as "survive").

For nine months beforehand I ran about 45 miles a week. Every Sunday morning Lisa and I would get up at 5:00 a.m. and do a long 13-mile trek that took us about two hours. In the past Sunday had been one of my two sleep-in mornings. Then Sabbath became my only brief haven of rest when I could luxuriate in bed past sunrise.

Of course, to be up by 5:00 on Sunday morning, I had to get to bed early . . . even on Saturday night. Gross! For all of my life Saturday night was the time you stayed up until the wee hours beating your friends at Trivial Pursuit or watching the late show on TV. All that I had to lay aside.

I've never smoked, so I haven't had the experience of "putting away" that hindrance. But out of 10,000 people who finish the marathon each March, you could probably count the smokers on the fingers of one hand. Tobacco and marathoning are mutually exclusive vices.

And it's rare to see a seriously overweight person making it up Sunset Boulevard in the marathon. The extra pounds are another thing you put away if you want to finish this particular race.

Apparently the author of Hebrews knew what he was talking about when he wrote: "Let us throw off everything that hinders and the sin that so easily entangles, and let us run with perseverance the race marked out before us" (Heb. 12:1, NIV).

Let's have this verse take us to a fourth reason for obedience, which I'll express this way: **The more we're emptied of sin and self, the more room we have for the Holy Spirit.**

For 40 years of pastoral service my dad's car trunk has been filled with missionary literature. Even though he's retired now, I'll bet he still has leftover Bible lessons in there going back to the Eisenhower administration, along with a broken slide projector, seven years' worth of back issues of the *Adventist Review,* a couple of *Youth's Instructors,* four tennis rackets, and a basketball that always needs pumping up. (He has four sons.)

The point is this: whenever he decides to fill up his trunk with something new, he has to clean out what's in there now. And if we truly want the Holy Spirit to fill and use our lives, then it becomes an experience of joy to do some emptying and make room for our new Guest.

Many leaders in today's evangelical world have tried to make the Holy Spirit their own personal servant. They hold services in which they command heaven's Valet to do their bidding. You know: "Name it and claim it." Or as it's more colorfully put: "Blab it and grab it." But in Garrie Williams' wonderful book *How to Be Filled by the Holy Spirit and Know It,* he makes this compelling observation: "We cannot use the Holy Spirit. The Holy Spirit is to use us." And if we want Him to use us, then we need to make room for Him somewhere in our lives.

I'm thankful that the Holy Spirit can start to use us beginning with His very first day on the job. If you've been a Christian only half an hour, the Holy Spirit has already taken up residence.

Back in 1992 I went to my daughter Kami's graduation at Monterey Bay Academy. One of the things that struck me was the juvenileness of some of the prayers the graduating seniors offered during the weekend services. Big blond six-foot-two surfer guys would get up in their mortarboards and maroon robes, with a big wad of gum in their mouths, and mumble, "Uh, dear Jesus, uh . . . thank You that we're, like, graduating and all. Thanks that our families can be here too. And [extremely long pause], uh, like, help us to have a good Sabbath today and, uh, everything. [Another long pause, accompanied by a spate of coughing from the rows of seniors.] Uh, Amen."

"What is this?" I muttered to my wife. "These guys are pathetic." For the next couple weeks I kept thinking to myself how much better I was at praying in public than the class of '92.

Jesus didn't hit me until much later with the realization that *God took those infant prayers, with all the "likes" and the gum chewing . . . and He honored them.* The Holy Spirit was using those kids. And pompous David B. Smith in the audience was too busy bragging on himself to notice.

Were they perfect prayers? No. But just imagine how many students the class pastor had to ask to pray before Surfer Sam finally nodded. "Yeah, man, I'll do it. I mean, like, I'm not too good or anything. But I'll try." He was willing, and the Holy Spirit enabled his efforts.

The Holy Spirit can take our stammering prayers—from all of us—and make them beautiful. He accepts our meager efforts at witnessing, our stumbling sermons, our rambling book manuscripts, and He makes good use of them somehow. And in the eyes of a perfect Father, my efforts are so little better than those of the MBA kids that I might as well just shut up about comparing us.

(I heard of a child who, when told that the sun is 93 million miles away from the earth, asked, "Is that from the upstairs window or the downstairs?" That's how much more spiritual I am than those academy seniors.)

Still, the Holy Spirit can use us *more* as we grow. Wouldn't you like to be used *more?* I have a sentence that's a regular part of my prayer life: "Lord, use me *all You can.* And do whatever it takes so that You *can* use me all You can."

At the Adventist Media Center different job opportunities have come along. I could do x or I could do y. (The ministries have really passed me around, trying to find one that would take me. "Look, Melashenko, it's your turn to have him for a while.") And I've always prayed, "God, put me where I can do the most for You. If it's a 'nine' here and a '10' over there, then show me." So far He's done pretty well at steering my ship.

And our lives are much like overloaded car trunks. Without a doubt, the sin in our lives gets in the way. It impedes the infilling of the Holy Spirit. Instead of doing much through us, He's held to small gains.

Prayerfully think with me how **deliberate sin** prevents the Holy Spirit from doing very much in your life. Or **wrong motives**. I'm glad He can make use of my good deeds done for the wrong reason, but talk about falling short!

Self-centeredness is another barrier. And of course, with a job in Christian media, it's been agonizing to see how abruptly a star mentality can end a person's witnessing potential. More about this in another chapter.

Then there's plain, unadulterated **unbelief**. All of these are messes in the trunk that shrink our effectiveness.

Let me pick out just one illustration. The subject of alcohol is a lively one these days as Christians of various faiths debate how "wine" ought to have been translated from the Hebrew and Greek and whether or not abstinence is a biblical principle.

But I just want to say this. A person who takes a drink—even *one* drink—is, in essence, saying to the Holy Spirit, "I'm taking a break from my contact with You. For the next three hours the phone's off the hook." Because when you've had any alcohol at all, your spiritual senses are the first thing to shut off. You can drink and sing, or drink and party, or drink and watch TV through the haze, but it's almost impossible to drink and then pray. Somehow the first taste severs your telephone connection to heaven.

So if you want to have the Holy Spirit filling you *more,* and if you want Him there all the time, then I believe you're going to think seriously about not having booze in the trunk of your car. And all sin, as we know, deadens the conscience, which is one of the specific avenues by which the Holy Spirit is present in our lives.

Dr. Ben Carson, author of the book *Gifted Hands,* describes his childhood struggle with a vicious temper. Once in the ninth grade he and a friend argued over what station the radio should be turned to. One thing led to another. He writes: "In that instant, blind anger—pathological anger—took possession of me. Grabbing the camping knife I carried in my back pocket, I snapped it open and lunged for the boy who had been my friend. With all the power of my young muscles, I thrust the knife toward his belly. The knife hit his big, heavy ROTC buckle with such force that the blade snapped and dropped to the ground. I stared at the broken blade and went weak. *I had almost killed him. I had almost killed my friend.*"

He then describes an agonizing personal battle with self that went on for hours. He wept alone in the tiny bathroom of his house, pleading and praying that God would take away his temper. A peace came over him as he sensed something changing inside his heart. "And since that day, since those long hours wrestling with myself and crying to God for help, I have never had a problem with my temper."

Consider how God has been able to *use* Dr. Carson since then. This remarkably talented neurosurgeon is one of the Holy Spirit's great vessels for service. The removal of that sin prepared the way for amazing achievements that honor God's name.

Bill Hybels, the senior pastor at Willow Creek Community church in Chicago, has accomplished some tremendous things for the Lord. I recently read his latest book, *Descending Into Greatness*, and it is an inspiring and Christ-centered challenge to service.

As my dad and I chatted about it later, I asked him, "How come Hybels has done so much? Why has his ministry thrived when others don't seem to go anywhere? What's made Willow Creek such a super church?"

"I don't know," my father mused. Himself a pastor, he's also watched with interest and admiration how God has used Bill Hybels. "Apparently he's just more on fire than most people, more dedicated." He went on to observe, in a way that I can't reproduce accurately here, how in his view Hybels has found the secret of self-emptying, of clearing away every hindrance to the Holy Spirit. And in his book *Descending* Hybels does describe some of the personal battles he's faced, where self needed to be swept away.

I love the title Dwight Nelson has coined to embody the attitude of a new generation of Adventists—"Radical Discipleship." They are Pioneer Memorial church Christians—and countless others around the globe—who will literally give up anything for the purpose of letting God use them. *Anything!* Anything in the trunk of the car that's in the way has got to go! Now! There's no waiting for a better time, no temporizing. "Well, I really ought to clean that stuff out. But maybe after the football season's over." None of that.

One of the great, wonderful, precious, unforgettable, most frequently underlined passages in the Bible can be found in Philippians 2. Verses 5 through 11 describe the "emptying" of Jesus, who made Himself nothing and became a servant. Read it a few times and sense what joy it is, then, for you and me to participate in giving Christ the exaltation described in those last three verses. "Every knee should bow," and "every tongue should confess"—and with rapturous pride and happiness.

Hebrews 1:9 describes how Jesus "loved righteousness" and so was anointed more than others. Used more than others . . . filled more than others . . . and accomplished so much more than others. Because He loved righteousness.

In Bible accounts fasting, prayer, *and* confession always precede the gift of the Holy Spirit. Garrie Williams suggests in his book that Christians ought to read prayerfully through the Ten Commandments on a regular basis, asking God to show us where sin is crowding out His Spirit. *Plead* with Him to show you.

I think with shame (and, to this day, some defensiveness) of the many times that grudges have held me back. How much good I could have accomplished during the accumulated hours and days I've spent in self-pity, in plotting vengeful speeches against people who had attacked me.

An old *M*A*S*H* TV episode had Hawkeye Pierce involved in some personal difficulties he was trying to keep private. But no matter where he went in the 4077th, everybody seemed to know all the juicy details. People had talked. Finally, in a burst of disgust, he called out in the mess hall, "How many of you are aware of all my intimate problems?" Virtually every hand went up.

And those kinds of turmoil and office politics can suck in so many people! One person resents another, retaliation sets in . . . and before you know it, the entire campus has taken sides. All the while the Holy Spirit must wait in sorrow on the sidelines, unable to be used or to use us.

The closer March 5, the date of the Los Angeles Marathon came, the more I wanted to be ready for it. The miles of practice went up, and the cookie allotment went down. As the date approached, my willingness to surrender pet treasures needed to heighten.

I've been reading Clifford Goldstein's book in which he describes his own moment of ultimate surrender. After years of working on a novel, the culmination of his dream, God spoke to him: "Cliff, you have been playing with Me long enough. If you want Me tonight, burn the novel."

What?

The message was unmistakable. And Clifford, who desperately wanted both the Lord and his best-selling novel, had to choose which to surrender. For the next two pages in his book the inward battle raged. *Please, Lord, anything but that . . .*

Finally, on page 87, he puts those manuscript pages (and only a writer can understand what it feels like even to *hold* that precious stack of 8½" x 11" sheets of paper in your hands) on the cold coils of his hot plate and turns it on. *All to Jesus I surrender . . .*

I shared with my friends in Wisconsin my conviction that there is very likely something *big* out there that we will all be called on to give up. Each of us may face a major moment of surrender ahead, a crossroad that will hurt. One for you, and one for me.

A Hollywood screenwriters' expression goes "You must kill all your darlings." Whatever little pet plot twist, joke, favorite line, treasured scene—if it doesn't work, if it doesn't fit in the overall movie, it's got to go. And killing those darlings is one of the agonies in the business.

William Goldman, a veteran in this field, describes how he had a scene he was absolutely dying to include in his screenplay for *Butch Cassidy and the Sundance Kid.* It was a clever little twist that he *had* to have—it sparkled with delightful irony.

But the stupid thing just didn't fit. No matter how he played with the scenes around it, this one always brought logic to a screeching halt. If he changed the beginning—well, then he might fit it in. But the picture would be inferior.

For days and weeks he tried on one scenario after another. But his one marvelous scene, his Oscar moment, just wouldn't go into the screenplay. All the mental shoehorns and crowbars in Hollywood wouldn't make it fit.

Finally, his heart in his throat, Goldman cut the scene out and threw it away. (It was before Macintosh wastebaskets on screenwriters' computer screens.) *Butch Cassidy* went on to become a commercial success—without the darling scene.

Friend, God is going to start pointing out our "darlings" to us—especially if we ask Him to. He doesn't ask us to obey in our own strength, but we need to be willing to obey.

My longtime friend and fellow writer for several happy It Is Written years, Martin Weber, uses the motel maid illustration. We may not be able to clean up the disastrous messes in our motel room, but we *do* need to be willing to hang that sign on the door: "Maid Service Requested." All those who have chosen to be radical disciples will make that decision.

I'm told that swimmers preparing for a major meet go through several days of what they call "peaking." As the race draws near, their swimming schedule intensifies to the point of agony, then cuts back. The last little bit right before a race they don't swim at all. Instead, they simply rest and deliberately *stew* about the upcoming event, allowing energy and drive and emotion to build up inside them until it reaches the explosive power of a volcano.

Then, the night before he steps up onto the starting blocks, a male swimmer will shave all the hair off his body for two reasons. First of all, for the added milliseconds of advantage he gets by being as streamlined as possible. But more important is the psychological effect. Those strokes of the razor, that very foreign act the night before he swims, reminds the athlete that he's willing to give up *everything*. "This is it, baby!"

Many years ago I read a great football book entitled *Instant Replay*, by Jerry Kramer, who played right guard for the Green Bay Packers. Jerry was a big guy, with his weight fluctuating around 250 during the season.

In order to keep his playing weight down to that level he would eat the tiniest little lunches. One little dish of peas, a very thin piece of meat, and some iced tea. Other players around him were chomping down on pieces of prime rib as big as footballs and topping it off with two pieces of apple pie with ice cream. It was sheer agony to be "in training" all season long. And who knows if that tiny edge he gained might ever pay off? You could win or lose every game by 40 points, reducing all your sacrifice to nothing.

But in the book's culminating big match against Dallas for the NFL Championship on December 31, 1967, the game—indeed, the season—came down to one block. The Packers, losing 17-14, had driven down to the Dallas one-foot line. With 16 seconds left in the game, Jerry Kramer had to block big Jethro Pugh and create a hole so quarterback Bart Starr could slip through for the victory. Two goal-line plays had already failed.

No time-outs left. Thirteen degrees below zero. The block of his life. And strong, mean, 245-pound Jerry Kramer poured everything within him into blocking Pugh out of the way.

Later he describes how sweet it was for the next two hours as TV sets around the country, on endless instant replays, showed player number 64 making that block and Bart Starr charging through the hole, plunging into the end zone for the score. "Block by Jerry Kramer," the announcers repeated again and again and again.

Peas and iced tea . . .

Are you willing? We sing "Fill My Cup, Lord"—which implies an earlier emptying. Are we willing, like Peter, to be hit over and over until we finally give up on self? He tried to walk on water. He made a blabbering fool of himself on the Mount of Transfiguration. He boasted of his own courage until the rooster crowed. It took three major hits, but Peter finally became an empty vessel the Holy Spirit could fill and use.

Why do we need constant infilling?" Garrie Williams asks. The answer is humorous and insightfully poignant. "Because we leak." Every day, every hour, we need Him so much.

And God longs to give Himself to us through the Spirit. It's His heart's greatest desire. Garrie describes his daughter's shriek of protest at seeing a little old lady from Pasadena driving sedately down the freeway—in a Corvette. What a waste of power! And God is eager to give us the full measure of the Spirit's power as we creep spiritually along.

Was all my effort worth that moment when I crossed the marathon? All the training and sacrifices and missed Saturday nights?

We're told by a reliable source that when we finally enter the kingdom of God, we are going to fling down our crowns at Jesus' feet and cry out: "Heaven is cheap enough!"

Let me borrow just one more quote from Jerry Kramer's book, a classic training line from Packers' coaching great Vince Lombardi. It has meaning for football players and radical disciples alike:

"Gentlemen, today we begin the big push."

CHAPTER SIX

The Jimmy Swaggart Fan Club

Let me try to pose the following question as gently and kindly as I can: Who in the world would want to have the job of senior recruiter for the Jimmy Swaggart Bible College?

As of this writing, JSBC is still operating somehow. It still has a faculty and some students in attendance. Every now and then, when I'm flipping through the TV channels in a motel room, Jimmy Swaggart's television program shows up. Some people still watch—and some people still send their money to Baton Rouge.

This probably does sound a little bit unkind—and I am sorry about that. But many people, Christians and columnists alike, have wondered aloud how anyone can seriously support a ministry so besmirched by open and defiant sin.

I'd like to consider in these next few pages a powerful two-edged sword. And here it is: **A life of sin-filled failure repels on-lookers, but a life of attractive righteousness draws them in.**

No one can ever deny that sin has a short-term lure. There is really such a thing as the pleasures of sin "for a season." People gravitate for a while around those who can curse the cleverest and drink the hardest. The biblical story of the prodigal son proves that. As long as he had money and free booze, people hung around. But the attraction never lasts.

In *How to Make Christianity Real* Morris Venden writes about a boyhood trip to the carnival. His dad didn't want him and his brother Louie to go, but he finally said, "You're old enough to make up your own minds."

"So we went to the carnival," Venden writes. "The first half was tremendous! Lots of fun! We spent our money like water. Tried everything. Then we began to get dizzy, sort of sick to our stomachs. And as we left the carnival that night, knowing that Father was home praying for us, we had discovered that *it was fun while it lasted, but it didn't last!*"

The "fun" of sin doesn't last. It's as temporary as those portable roller-coaster rides at the carnival. Today we find neon and cotton candy and whirring engines and the shrieks of the crowd. Tomorrow it's an empty cow pasture. And the world around us fills to overflowing with anxious, restless people on an endless search for another thrill, another partner, another chemical jolt.

But the day eventually comes when tired people demand, "Doesn't anyone around here have a life that is working for them? Is there someone, somewhere, who is experiencing quiet victory?"

Ah . . . that's where our opportunity arrives! A text my brother Dan likes to preach from comes to mind: "Thanks be to God, who always leads us in triumphal procession in Christ **and through us spreads everywhere the fragrance of the knowledge of Him**" (2 Cor. 2:14, NIV). That life of quiet obedience, of subdued, unflashy success, has the sweet aroma that will bring people to our doorstep.

Elizabeth J. Guetschow interviewed conservative columnist Cal Thomas in the June 1994 edition of *Religious Broadcasting* magazine. A former Moral Majority lieutenant, Thomas, who hosts a talk show on CNBC, recently began to write a column that appears in secular newspapers. The interview article, appropriately titled "Life Outside the Catacombs," focused on his "journey beyond Christianity's safe circles."

One of his comments bears mention here. "The unsaved are not interested in your doctrine," Thomas observes. "They're interested in whether it works out in your life. Are you still married to your spouse, for example? A lot of Christians are getting divorces and writing books justifying it; that's not going to cut it to the unsaved.

Also, certain denominations major in the minors. This just doesn't appeal to the world. I don't drink alcohol for a number of reasons, but I've never had anybody come up to me in a restaurant and say, 'Pardon me, I noticed you're drinking a diet Coke. Would you tell me what I must do to be saved?' They don't care what's in my glass; they care what's in my heart."

Let me say it again. Hungry people everywhere are looking in desperation for men and women who exhibit the fragrance of natural obedience. "Does loving God work for anybody?" they question plaintively.

It's painful even to wonder aloud how many millions of people have left the church—or never even walked in the front door—because of the unchanged lives of those inside. C. S. Lewis, in his *Mere Christianity*, writes with controlled anguish about those who look at the petty meanness of some "stupid and unsatisfactory" Christian and then harrumph, "So there's your boasted new man. Give me the old kind!"

Adventist author Dan Day wrote a piece a few years ago entitled "The Myth of the Wandering Seeker After Truth" in which he insightfully exposed the false concept that people are roaming the streets of our planet intently wondering about what's the right day to worship, what the state of the dead really is, and how the 2300 days come out. People don't care about that stuff! What they want to know is Do your beliefs make a difference in your life? Are you happier? Are you kinder? Are you a better neighbor, a more loyal spouse, an improved performer at the workplace? Do you have peace when they don't?

A couple years ago I was reading *The Kingdom of the Cults*, by the late Walter Martin. He stoutly defends Seventh-day Adventism as *not* being a cult, but then spends almost 100 pages graciously pointing out what he feels are mistakes in Adventist theology.

I'm a big boy, so I tried to wade through it. But I'm not a real big boy—at least in theological training. The only Greek I know is what I picked up in my PUC calculus class. (And I got B-minuses in that.)

So some of his hairsplitting arguments against the Adventist doctrine of Sabbath observance were above me. He had an impressive little pile of texts and debate points. Some seemed patently weak to me, while others made a certain sense.

As I thought about it later, it struck me that he had a pile . . . and we had a pile. Two piles of texts, one on each side of this friendly battlefield. I was still thankful for Adventist truth—still a believer—but I certainly had to concede that the discussion had two sides to it. Two piles.

It struck me later that *my friends and neighbors didn't care two cents about either pile!* It meant little to the students in my college algebra class whether "the Lord's day" in Revelation 1:10 refers to Saturday or Sunday. Is Romans 14:5, 6 a commentary on the Sabbath or just Jewish feast days? *They don't care!* Nobody I know is even thinking about that stuff. They want to know, How can I pay my bills? How can I get my girlfriend to move back in with me? How can I pile up enough test points so that Professor Smith will let me skip the final?

The one thing neighbors and onlookers care about is this: "What does observing Sabbath do in your life? Is all that extra time with God making you sweeter and more loving? Are you the best neighbor on the block? Are you the best math teacher we ever had?"

Speaking of math, from a "proportion" point of view, if an Adventist spends 24 hours with God while the average Sundaykeeper just goes to church on Sunday for three hours and then uses the rest of the day for secular pursuits—wouldn't you expect the Adventist to be *eight times* as Spirit-filled? Eight times as caring and friendly? Eight times as unselfish and giving?

OK, so we're sleeping for eight of those hours? That reduces the ratio to 16:3 . . . or still, let's say, five times as nice. How about it?

The Vineyard Christian Fellowship congregation rents our Thousand Oaks Adventist Church each Sunday. On several occasions, particularly around holidays, we've gotten together and enjoyed some joint worship services. (It was fascinating to see them washing SDA members' feet for the first time.)

But I had to confess to myself that these Christians were just as nice as our own people. We *weren't* 5.33 times as loving and spiritually dedicated as they were. It looked to be pretty much a dead-even tie when it came to Christian love.

Now, I don't think we've just destroyed the validity of Sabbath observance. I still believe in that pillar of truth. But I have to concede two points: (1) as far as interested onlookers are concerned, we've not gained any "advantage" in the one area in which they're looking for a winner; and (2) we've not yet allowed the Sabbath to transform us as I believe it can.

But the Christian who allows the Sabbath to make him or her a beautiful, obedient believer has got something special. Watchers searching for high quality will find themselves drawn to that individual.

Examples are numerous, and we all have our favorites. Lisa and I were both touched last year by reading *Through the Shadowlands*, about C. S. Lewis's brief and painful romance with Joy Davidman. The book and two feature films have explored how intense beliefs and Christian ardor brought two people together in a love experience few of us will ever know. And that story captivated multiplied thousands of readers and filmgoers. "Mere" Christianity was made to be the most beautiful and lasting thing in the world.

Consider Mother Teresa. Only a small fraction of society has any inkling what her core doctrinal positions are. Yet she is universally admired. People have a higher opinion of Christianity because of her life and her actions.

It Is Written's Mark Finley loves to talk about his father, James, who is a quiet, wonderful man. Back when Mark was a teenager his father was the only Adventist Christian in the family. Always gracious, always kind, never preaching or pushy, he was unfailingly cheerful about praising his wife's great cooking (as he quietly left the pork chops for others in the family). He would volunteer to drive Mark to Friday night dances and basketball games, and then go over to the church for his own meeting. "I'll pick you up at 10:00, OK, son?"

And after a while it made an impact. That kind of loving obedience to Jesus eventually won Mark to the truth. Thousands today have come to know Jesus as a result.

But the challenge is not only to have an experience in righteousness with God but to be able to share it winsomely. Talk about difficult!

A refrain often finds its way into my prayers. "Lord, help me not to be a nut." And it's largely because of the two-edged sword of *influence* that I say it.

Nobody's attracted to the kind of unbalanced, wild-eyed Christianity that's all too visible in the world around us. How many people have looked at the antics of Christians and said to themselves, "Huh?"

On several occasions when I've come out of Dodger Stadium late at night, a man with a megaphone has been determined to share his Christian experience with everyone who scoots past him. It's a rambling, almost incoherent, diatribe, filled with King James Version texts strung together and punctuated by electronic megaphone squeals and "Shut up, stupid!"s. Fans almost trample each other scurrying to get away from the sermon, which is usually on the topic "The Final Judgment and Hell and All of You Are Going There." And for some reason, guys like that are always out there on a losing night. The Dodgers have just been creamed, so the exiting fans are already surly and out of sorts.

How can we do better?

First of all, we need to have an experience with Christ that is genuine and real. After 10 years in Christian television I've come to realize that anybody can read off a TelePrompTer. You can prop just about anyone up in front of that electronic screen and have him or her read John 3:16 to the masses. But we need an experience that is real. Thank God for our Mark Finleys and Lonnie Melashenkos who have a daily walk with their Lord. Their broadcasted words and their private lives are in sync.

I remember back in 1987 when somebody sent me two tickets to a fund-raising dinner for a leading televangelist who was thinking of running for president. Out of curiosity, Lisa and I drove down to Anaheim to see what it was all about.

Just as we entered a huge banquet hall, the candidate walked in, just a few feet away from us. Several "advance men" milled all around him, carrying walkie-talkies and other paraphernalia. Right on cue, one of them began to holler in a loud voice: "Run, Pat, run! Run, Pat, run!" The crowd took up the "spontaneous" chant, which soon echoed through the hall.

Some TV cameras were just then being set up, and I watched with interest as the next little bit of political drama took place. Again on cue, the candidate walked up to a leading political figure. Just as the electronic red lights flicked on he put on a big smile, and the two men embraced right in front of the cameras like long-lost bosom friends. "3—2—1—*hug!*" I had never seen "staging" like this before, and the unreality of this Christian campaign left me a little bit shaken.

The story is told of a man who wrote a letter to an airline executive complaining that the plane was dirty on his latest flight. Just a few days later he got a very gracious and humble apology from a vice president of the company. What a shame, the official lamented. How could such a thing have happened? He was so very sorry.

The vice president went on to assure the writer that every possible step had been taken. The crew involved had been reprimanded. The entire plane was going into the hangar for an extended cleaning. All the seats and carpeting would be removed and shampooed. The company was going to rewrite its employee manual completely and upgrade its policies to make sure such a mistake would never happen again.

"Wow!" the recipient of the letter whistled to himself. "I'm impressed. These people mean business!"

Then he noticed something else in the envelope. By mistake his original complaint letter had been tucked in with the corporate reply. Along the margin of the letter the airline VP had scrawled, "Send this idiot our usual clean-airplane letter."

Doesn't that break your heart? And do we perhaps see our phony selves in there somewhere?

Dale Carnegie tells the following story in his book *How to Win Friends and Influence People:*

"I was waiting in line to register a letter in the post office at Thirty-third Street and Eighth Avenue in New York. I noticed that the registry clerk was bored with his job—weighing envelopes, handing out the stamps, making change, issuing receipts—the same monotonous grind year after year. So I said to myself: 'I am going to try to make that chap like me. Obviously, to make him like me, I must say something nice, not about myself, but about him.' So I asked myself, 'What is there about him that I can honestly admire?' That is sometimes a hard question to answer, especially with strangers; but in this case, it happened to be easy. I instantly saw something I admired to no end.

"So while he was weighing my envelope, I remarked with enthusiasm: 'I certainly wish I had your head of hair.'

"He looked up, half-startled, his face beaming with smiles. 'Well, it isn't as good as it used to be,' he said modestly. I assured him that although it might have lost some of its pristine glory, nevertheless it was still magnificent. He was immensely pleased. We carried on a pleasant little conversation, and the last thing he said to me was: 'Many people have admired my hair.'

"I'll bet that chap went out to lunch that day walking on air. I'll bet he went home that night and told his wife about it. I'll bet he looked in the mirror and said: 'It is a beautiful head of hair.'"

The kicker to the story comes later when Carnegie describes how he related this incident in public and a man immediately asked him, "What did you want to get out of him?"

Through the entire book Carnegie insists that what he is talking about is not a flattery game or self-serving manipulation. "Nice hair!" "Great car, boss!" "Good job on that report." What he is talking about is a whole new viewpoint, a whole new way of life.

Dale Carnegie had learned how to truly appreciate people, how to have an attitude of love and optimism and praise at all times. It was no game to him, but a God-given new way of life.

I wish I could tell you how many times godly people have strengthened my Christian experience. Royce Williams, one of my close friends both from mission field days and in recent years at It Is Written, is a cheerful and genuine Christian. I recall once being with him as we visited with a woman who was having real emotional struggles.

Royce's face softened. "Why don't we pray right now?" he asked her. "I'd really like to pray for you." With utter spontaneity and warmth he prayed briefly, asking God to "bless this sister of mine."

There was nothing contrived about it, nothing put-on. No reporters lurked nearby to catch it. The It Is Written's camera crew was nowhere in sight. Royce just reached out, instinctively, from years of habit, and called on his heavenly Friend. I love that!

The very first time I met Pastor Mark Finley was back in 1984. Someone asked me to pick Mark up at the San Francisco airport on an 11:50 p.m. flight. "How will I know you, Pastor Finley?" I asked him on the phone.

"Call me Mark." He laughed. "I'll be the skinniest guy off the plane . . . and I'll have a Sabbath school quarterly in my hand."

With those twin identifying marks I had no problem finding him. Collecting his bags, we began driving toward Leoni Meadows, our Adventist youth camp in northern California.

We got to our motel around 2:00 in the morning knowing that we had to get up again at 5:00 in order to get Mark there for his 7:00 a.m. speaking appointment. (This is the kind of schedule the man keeps.) By 2:01 I had fallen into bed, wearily determined to grab as much of that three-hour chunk of sleep as I could.

Not Mark. Even at 2:00 in the morning (5:00 a.m. for a Michigan preacher's body clock), he got out his Bible and read for 10 minutes. No big fuss—he just quietly did it.

I forced my eyes open at 5:00 in the morning, only to discover that Mark had gotten up 10 minutes earlier and read his Bible some more. Now, what kind of Christian, with only three hours to sleep after a transcontinental flight, would have a devotional experience on *both* ends of that chunk of time? Unbelievable! And what an influence in my life. I'm telling you, hang around with people like that. It'll do you some good.

Even during my week at the Wisconsin camp meeting I experienced examples of godly influence. Pastor Clint Meharry, who was in charge of the young adult tent, was a real blessing. I still can remember one of his prayers on my behalf just before we went up onto the platform together. "Bless Dave, dear Father. Feed us through what You give him tonight." What solid strength comes from the prayers of a fellow Christian!

My dad, who was a rather shaky Adventist kid at La Sierra

College back in the 1940s, has his own story to tell. His major was theology, but his minor was in shooting spitwads from the balcony during chapel. Harmless fun, perhaps, but the spitwads were a surface symptom of deeper confusion.

Dad has often told me how an older student sat down next to him one day. "Ken . . . man, how's it going? I'm worried about you." Nothing patronizing or holier-than-thou—just a kind and godly man being a natural influence. A quiet one-to-one sermon. "I'm praying for you." And that was a turning point. Dad went on to become a dedicated missionary.

As we close this chapter, let me point you toward a challenge: **Touch as many lives as you can.** Be fragrant with the gospel in as many places as possible. Get out of your ghetto and be the salt of the earth *in* the earth to as many people as you can.

And think of the thousands and maybe millions of times that people in conversations may consider Sunday legislation and other various kinds of persecution for the people of God. "But wait a minute!" one will interject. "I know an Adventist! I had one for a neighbor in my last town. *He* wasn't like that. Those people aren't the 'enemies of God,' like they're saying on the news. A beautiful Christian, he was a real friend."

Touch as many lives as you can right now. I considered it a divinely sent privilege in 1992 to be elected the president of the Religious Public Relations Council, a 500-plus group of religious communicators from all faith groups. For two years I was able to travel and meet many of them. My president's column appeared in the quarterly newsletter. At the national conventions they handed me the gavel and asked me to preside.

More than once fellow members who were the top PR officers for their entire denominations came up and confided to me, "David, you're the first Adventist we ever knew."

Believe me, I tried to observe my Sabbath and order my vegetarian meals in a way that exuded attractive kindness and winsome "fragrance."

Let's return back to Jimmy Swaggart for a minute. I don't know him, and it's unlikely that any reader of this book does.

But we don't know what he's been through. None of us have been in his position. We have no idea of his temptations or his past or the inner variables that may have brought him to his knees in failure.

My daughter Kami, who is a very casual housekeeper, has on her dormitory room wall an Ellen White quote. "In all our associations it should be remembered that in the experience of others there are chapters sealed from mortal sight. On the pages of memory are sad histories that are sacredly guarded from curious eyes. There stand registered long, hard battles with trying circumstances, perhaps troubles in the home life, that day by day weaken courage, confidence, and faith" (*The Ministry of Healing,* p. 158).

I recently read two books by Richard Dortch, the former PTL director who spent some time in prison for his mistakes. He writes with genuine love about Jim Bakker, also an inmate, and the hidden pain that some of us don't know about. There were things about that story that were kept from our view. And before we write books with too-loud sneers regarding fallen sinners, we need to stop and remember that only God has the pages that may have been torn from the story before we picked it up.

The only story I know is mine. All I can know and all I can say is that *I* want to be used by God as one of His fragrant vessels. Instead of a yellow sign outside my office that says "Men at Work," I want it to read "Love at Work."

Except that anyone can print up a sign. Anyone can adopt a slogan such as "the caring church." Anyone can read "I love you" off a cue card on Christian television. I want it to be real. I want it to be genuine and as spontaneous as breathing.

In 1992 George Bush faced a Republican challenger who ran what some pundits called a "nose out of joint" campaign. The politician seemed to attract only angry Americans. His supporters weren't happy unless they weren't happy.

What a challenge, instead, to draw people who are looking for quiet victory, for infectious cheerfulness. People are watching us. Will they see love in us?

CHAPTER SEVEN

"Lean on Me, Baby"

He is a screen-filling mass of masculine muscle and virility—at least in his own mind. Comic actor/writer/director Woody Allen has made himself a millionaire by poking fun at his own scrawny homeliness and clumsy boastfulness around women.

In one of his early films, *Play It Again, Sam,* he tries to play a supportive tough-guy romantic ally to Diane Keaton. Woody has just fallen in love with Diane, who is married to his best friend. It's a complicated mess, and she moans aloud about the tangled web of relationships.

He adjusts his crooked glasses and juts out his chin as the two of them make their way up the stairs leading to his house. "Lean on me, baby," he growls, trying not to let his voice squeak. Just as he utters the words he trips on his own shoelace and almost pitches over the side into the thornbushes. It's Diane who has to reach out and rescue *him*.

To recap up to this point, we have discovered these positive blessings that stem from obedience: (1) we "grow" in our relationship with Christ; (2) we honor God (Matt. 5:16); (3) we love Jesus and copy His life; (4) we're filled more by the Holy Spirit; and (5) we draw others in.

Now we can add a sixth: **We strengthen God's church as His pil-**

lars through obedience. We become the ones others can lean on.

As I said in the first chapter, being good does so much—but it doesn't save. Obedience is a tremendous thing in a Christian's life, but it does not earn salvation. It never has been and it never will be the ticket to heaven.

All obedience is a gift from God, accomplished through His power. Justification is a gift from God. Sanctification is a gift from God. It's all Jesus. As H.M.S. Richards used to say, "Jesus only."

I told my Wisconsin young adults group that these discussions were somewhat like a boat trip. There is a lighthouse called "Righteousness by Faith." And we may sail our little boat in the waters surrounding that lighthouse, finding nine (or so) good reasons to be good. Our little journeys may give us some interesting discoveries about the benefits of obedience.

"But I never want to get very far away from that lighthouse!" I declared. And I meant it. The doctrine of grace must always be within our sights—without any need for spiritual binoculars. Both salvation and obedience are God's gifts to His grateful people.

Luke 22 shares one of the most beautiful challenges found in the Bible. Jesus and His 12 disciples are in the upper room having their final Passover feast; Gethsemane and Calvary lie just ahead. And Jesus has just delivered a very kind sermon in response to the oft-repeated argument over who should be the greatest? In verse 27 He declares, "I am among you as one who serves" (NIV).

And then He turns to Peter. "Simon, Simon, Satan has asked to sift you as wheat. But I have prayed for you, Simon, that your faith may not fail. And when you have turned back, **strengthen your brothers**" (verses 31, 32, NIV).

"I have prayed for you, Simon." What a marvelous announcement to hear that Jesus is praying for *you!* And then those words: "Strengthen your brothers. They're going to need you." Jesus tells Peter to be a pillar that others can lean on in a precarious world.

How very *opposite* from the "I am greatest" campaign. Jesus wants us for His humble pillars. Pillars somebody can find support and strength from.

"When you have turned back . . ." Peter's denial of his Lord still lay ahead. That very night, in fact. The proud fisherman still had a kind of obedience to learn before he could be a pillar to the rest. But the events of that Thursday through Sunday did indeed begin to make Peter a rock the others could depend upon.

I have mentioned pillars in my life. People such as my dad. My "bosses" at the Adventist Media Center—godly, spiritual men such as Lonnie Melashenko and Mark Finley. I could call them at 4:00 a.m. for help if necessary. Wonderful Adventist women I have worked with—Elaine Dodd and Pauline Mostert. What a blessing such obedient Christians are as friends I can lean on. There are stories I would never relate in a book—quiet, personal moments when they carried me through times of great travail.

On many occasions fellow writers Martin Weber and Steve Mosley would join me for prayer. Nothing can compare with a time like that. Now I enjoy the same with my VOP associate, John McLarty. He comes into my office around quitting time with his effusive grin, sweater, and scuffed-up shoes. "Dave, we've got to pray!" he informs me. "Turn off that stupid computer!"

God has always had great pillars. Consider how Abraham sustained his own small nation. Hundreds, thousands, leaned on him.

Or Esther. The entire Jewish population placed its national trust in her. "Who knoweth," Mordecai challenged her, "whether thou art come to the kingdom for such a time as this?" (That's great in the King James Elizabethan English, isn't it?)

In both cases, and in so many others, it was *obedience* that gave these champions their status as pillars to the people. Abraham and Esther obeyed, and countless others found refuge in that obedience. The same with Joseph, Daniel, and the rest of Scripture's long list.

I have a soft spot in my heart for the World War II-type of Adventist-hero story in which a hero rises to the occasion. John Weidner of *Flee the Captor* fame. Eric Liddell (*Chariots of Fire*), who was a tower of strength in his prison camp. The brave missionaries described in the classic SDA book *Behind Barbed Wire*. Of all those interned in that Japanese prison camp, it was the missionaries—Adventists and others—who often stepped forward and carried the others through to survival. God's people were the champions who organized work details, set up church services, and sustained the weak and suffering among them. It was the missionaries who stood up to the Japanese commandant, setting moral boundaries that even he dared not cross.

Maximilian Kolbe was a Catholic priest who suffered with countless others in a World War II concentration camp. Kolbe was the champion, the pillar, a titan of strength to those who were weaker.

And when the horrible day came that the Nazis announced that 10 men chosen at random were to die as a penalty for an attempted escape, it was Kolbe who quietly stepped forward and said politely to the commanding officer, "I would like to die in this man's place. He has a wife and children. I have none."

Some religious systems seem to emphasize loneness, the practice of solitary meditation and the individual's progress toward Paradise. Thank God the Christian faith is different. Christianity has always been intended to be a *fellowship* of believers. "And let us consider how we may spur one another on toward love and good deeds. Let us not give up meeting together, as some are in the habit of doing, but let us encourage one another—and all the more as you see the Day approaching" (Heb. 10:24, 25, NIV).

Tony Evans, cofounder and senior pastor of Oak Cliff Bible Fellowship in Dallas and author of *The Victorious Christian Life*, points to Ephesians 4 as a powerful command for Christians to support one another through fellowship. He concludes: "Our relationship to the corporate body of Christians is crucial to the progress of the growth of our personal relationship with God."

As I mentioned earlier, Lisa and I have a resolve that is just ours. I'm not here to push it on you, but let me express it here again: **We're determined that, 52 weeks a year, we'll be in church together.** Both of us need the strengthening influence of being in church with friendly pillars. And both of us want to be friendly pillars, and you can't do that if you're home in bed or out paddling a canoe somewhere.

Even at the Adventist Media Center I've seen enough examples of people who were determined to be a Christian all by themselves. But it doesn't work. "Closet Christianity" is a proven failure. It invariably leads to selfishness and fanciful interpretations of truth.

The evening before I shared this chapter topic with my friends in Wisconsin, the NBC network aired a rerun of the TV movie *Deadly Deception: The David Koresh Story*. Ouch! What a painful lesson that tears at the heart of Adventists.

It really is a deadly deception—with thanks to NBC for the appropriate title—when people think they can go off by themselves and establish a healthy religion. "We want our own little compound, our own Waco Wonderland, where we can be left alone." Sooner or later, that separatist mentality brings one to the point of guns, grape Kool-aid, and then ashes.

But this book is about goodness. What's the connection?

Open sin in the church, and especially in the life of one of the church's pillars, saps the strength of the whole body. Think how scandals and divorces have brought down some of the mighty trees among the people of God.

King David was a pillar in Israel. Then came the pain of Bathsheba-gate. The entire nation paid a price for his personal follies. Second Samuel 24 describes how, when David ordered a census taken of his military forces, the three punishment options from the Lord included (1) three years of famine, (2) three months of military oppression from enemies, or (3) three days of plague in the land.

Three choices . . . and each one involved pain that the whole kingdom would have to bear. David finally concluded, "I am in deep distress. Let us fall into the hands of the Lord, for his mercy is great; but do not let me fall into the hands of men" (verse 14, NIV). And the Lord's mercy is great—but 70,000 innocent people still died in the plague.

Richard Nixon's funeral in 1994 reminded us how the sins of a few can affect a nation. Watergate very nearly poisoned the entire American system. Gerald Ford didn't mince words when he took office on August 9, 1974. "Our long national nightmare is over." A pillar, a head of state, had failed to live up to the public trust. He had let down all those middle-class Americans—"the Silent Majority"—who were supposedly the Nixon constituency.

And to be politically fair, I have to observe that every president's mistakes cost the country. Whether Republican, Democrat, Libertarian, or Whig (I'm thinking of joining the latter party), a mistake in the Oval Office affects us even way out here in Newbury Park, California.

I hit my Wisconsin friends pretty hard with the following challenges:

Think how much we need people in our churches who are quietly obedient to Christ—**pillars we know we can lean on.**

How could we have treasurers if we didn't know they were honest and prudent?

How could we have leaders in our youth divisions if we couldn't find people who exhibited marital faithfulness? Man, I've got daughters in there!

We need people who understand the concept of true Sabbath joy to plan our worship services. Where are the pillars who love to worship, who live and breathe worship? Here at Thousand Oaks we have Warren and Jan Judd and Paulette Straine and Ralph Figueroa. They love to worship the Lord! They get together on Friday night and plan praise music that is joy-filled and Christ-centered and reverent and consistent with the pastor's theme for that Sabbath. Each of them will work for hours to integrate the music in a "presentation" computer program so that every worshiper can joyfully participate. And they enjoy doing it. How could we survive and thrive without pillars like these?

Friends, what would we do without pillars **who understand the gospel?** Who would teach our lesson study classes if we didn't have strong men and women who love the righteousness-by-faith message? We need that in every single division from cradle roll right up to the seniors discussion class. That's one pillar we need real bad.

Our families need pillars—dads and moms who are strong in Jesus, who are obedient. Hey, haven't you ever sung this song before: "With Jesus in the daddy's heart, happy, happy home"? And if He isn't there?

It's especially great when our young adults catch the vision of being Adventist pillars. And of course, I made a big point of saying so in Wisconsin. What a blessing when a newlywed couple in their early 20s decide to be pillars in the church.

Too often our believers make up their minds when they're a creaky 70 years of age that it's time to become a pillar. Thank God for our seventy-something champions, but where were you when we needed you these past several decades? A young person who decides to be strong in the body of Christ can give 40 or 50 years of helpful service.

During a recent summer the Cle Elum Adventist Church in Washington invited me to give a parenting seminar. Before I arrive at such appointments I always check into a church's membership figures because it's tough to give a good program to a tiny little knot of seven or eight dozing participants. The Washington Conference directory told me that Cle Elum had about 100 members on the books.

I winced when I saw that. One hundred "book" members usually translates into maybe 50-60 who actually attend church. And out of that, 15 or 20 people might fall into the "parenting" age span—and who knows how many of that number might show up? Seven or eight dozing participants.

When I got there I discovered the church was about as small as I had been envisioning. But much to my surprise, people just kept rolling in. Twenty . . . 30 . . . 35 . . . 40 . . .

"What's going on?" I asked one of them. "Who are all these people? Visiting friends from the Presbyterian Church? Sinners from the highways and byways?"

Turns out they were all members. Cle Elum, with maybe 100 members on the books, is packed to the rafters with young adults—*all* of them active. When there's a program or a seminar, they all come. Alive for the Lord, they're *all* pillars. Wow! (And talk about a fun seminar that night!)

But sometimes even just *one* pillar can make an enormous difference for the Lord. Even if you're in the proverbially dead church where people rent ice skates to go down the center aisle, you can change things. One strong person can turn a church around.

A few years ago Pastor Gordon Bietz gave one of the best sermons I have ever heard. It borrowed the theme song from the popular TV sitcom *Cheers,* a song that stresses the idea that people want to go where everyone knows their name. One character, Norm Peterson, would walk into the bar each evening just to hear all the regular patrons call out his name.

Well, let me just say that people shouldn't have to go into a Boston bar in order to be loved. They should be able to get that love, that acceptance, at local Adventist churches. And millions of people would start coming if even *one* person "knew their name." You can make a difference.

Baseball fans recognize that one effective player who's "hot" can carry the whole team for a while. One Mr. October can take a team through the play-offs and World Series. And in the church, even one key player who loves the Saviour and whose life of obedience radiates acceptance and love can carry the congregation. Not forever, to be sure, but one Mr. October usually sparks excellence and some good clutch hitting in other players before too many games go by.

We hear a lot of preaching at camp meeting about "the remnant church." Coming as I do from a public relations background—and working closely as I have for years with Christians from non-Adventist backgrounds—I work my way around that expression with real caution. It is difficult to worship with a Baptist friend at his church and attend his deeply spiritual Sunday school class, and yet mutter to myself on the way out, "Doesn't matter. *We're* still the remnant church."

Perhaps from a PR perspective our GC president has found an even better way to express this belief: "The Seventh-day Adventist Church was called into existence by God *to do the work of the remnant.*" I like that very much.

During my recent two-year term as president of the Religious Public Relations Council I once had the honor of addressing the Washington, D.C., chapter of RPRC. In fact, they held their luncheon meeting at our SDA General Conference headquarters (and raved about the vegetarian meal arranged for them by Shirley Burton, who, by the way, is one of our denomination's most talented communicators in dealing with our brothers and sisters of other faiths).

In my brief remarks to them I confessed that we as Adventists sometimes feel that we must finish the work all by ourselves. "Populations are growing so fast," I lamented, "and we sometimes feel that we are hopelessly falling behind."

But then I added this—and I hope my readers will understand. "Too often we forget that over in Russia, for example, we are getting some very good help from the Baptists. We're trying to reach millions for Jesus Christ, and the Baptists are there helping to shoulder that load. Presbyterians are in all corners of the world just as we are, picking up their share of the mandate established by the gospel commission of Matthew 28. I'm glad we're not alone out there," I said. "And forgive us when we have thought that we were."

Having said that to *them*, let me say *this* to *you*: **We do have a special message!** I believe it's God's will that in the last days many will come from the Baptist Church into our special truths—and not vice versa. Millions will flock from the Catholic fold into the full light of Adventist fellowship. That is God's plan.

Sadly we hear much criticism of the leadership in the Seventh-day Adventist Church. And it's unjustified criticism. It's wrongly placed. You can hear the mean jabs and complaints at camp meeting; you encounter it in the unwanted mailings that keep flooding our mailboxes. Friends, these are satanic attacks.

The many conference leaders I have met are pillars! I've listened to their prayers. I've seen them wrestle with God, entreating Him for guidance in tough decisions. I know union presidents and other leaders on that level and have seen them operate—they are pillars too. Robert Folkenberg is a strong and gracious pillar. Again, I've heard him pray and heard him express his heartfelt love for Jesus and for this church. His appearances on *It Is Written* have been spiritual highlights for the broadcast. Praise God for these great Adventist pillars that we can all lean on.

By comparison, I'm just a little frog in the pond. But I'd like to be a pillar too. I'd like to be obedient so that someone who needs a friend, someone out there who is "one of the least of these," my brothers and sisters, can lean on me.

CHAPTER EIGHT

A Confession From "Little Smith"

Humor columnist Art Buchwald often serves as my spiritual adviser (though he doesn't know it). In an old column entitled "The Good and the Bad" he describes a conversation with his young son they had after seeing a World War II movie. The son raises the question of why the Russians were good during the war and bad now (this was during the cold war period), while the Germans were bad during the war and good now. Then they struggle with the difference between the people of East and West Germany. When the boy cannot grasp the concept of shifting allegiances, the idea that our Germans are good, while the Soviet Union's East Germans are bad, Buchwald replies, "Well, it doesn't make any difference if you understand it or not. . . . Everyone else does. I never saw a kid who asked so many silly questions."

Isn't that the dumbest thing you ever heard in your life? "Our Germans are good—theirs are bad"?

Here's the heartbreaking point behind the humorous jabs, though: **Sin has a terrible power to divide.** That's where all this "good-bad" thinking comes from.

Let's go back to the Garden of Eden. Eve disobeyed God, and division was the instant result. The Blame Game Super Bowl started that very afternoon. "It was this woman You gave me. What'd You have to make her for?"

Why Be Good?

You can go down a checklist of those things that divide us as a nation. Or you can pick your own favorite examples—but every time you will find sin as the agent of disunity.

Consider John Howard Griffin's best-selling book on racism, *Black Like Me*. A White journalist writing in the 1950s, he made his skin black and traveled the Deep South, experiencing the agonies and the shame of hate and prejudice. He walked for miles to find a restroom someone would let him use. In fact, he and his fellow Blacks would have to plan their entire day around available facilities. Often he would experience the "hate stare," a gaze of cold disgust that seemed to say, "Why don't you get off our planet?"

Later in his account Griffin traveled to Mississippi on a Greyhound bus, always in the back. Often the driver would not let him off at the announced rest stops. He hitchhiked and suffered verbal abuse and an ugly sexual curiosity from the White men who picked him up.

The coup de grace came when a young Black man offered him a place to stay for the night. Out on the very edges of poverty and squalor he received a clean spot on the floor of a two-room cabin.

But Griffin could not sleep. The horrors of the day had simply been too much. Finally he went outside and sat in the cold Mississippi night air on an overturned washtub. And wept. "I thought of my daughter, Susie, and of her fifth birthday today, the candles, the cake and party dress; and of my sons in their best suits. They slept now in clean beds in a warm house while their father, a bald-headed old Negro, sat in the swamps and wept, holding it in so he would not awaken the Negro children." Griffin wept over the evil hatred caused by sin.

Sin. Separation. They've been bedfellows now for thousands of long years.

I wrote in a previous book, *Heaven*, about some of the racist-tinged TV ads that appeared during the 1988 presidential campaign and how they split the electorate. On his deathbed political guru Lee Atwater confessed his wrongdoing. Sin had brought division—and he was repentant.

Of course, we can look within our own ranks and see how a

church can experience the shattering separation that sin always brings. Every time we have a General Conference session, it seems, you can find those people who are out on the sidewalks instead of inside the meeting arena. Their protest signs and their "video presentations" decry the sin in our midst—but it's their own strategies that add fuel to the fires of controversy and separation.

What a contrast with what Christ has always prayed for us to experience—especially in these last days. "My prayer is not for them [the disciples] alone. I pray also for those who will believe in me through their message, that all of them may be one, Father, just as you are in me and I am in you. May they also be in us so that the world may believe that you have sent me" (John 17:20, 21, NIV).

Ellen White comments: "This most touching and wonderful prayer reaches down the ages" (*Patriarchs and Prophets*, p. 520). Those three sentences pouring from the heart of our Redeemer are to be applied to the Adventist Church *in the late 1990s*. They are for *right now*.

I had to give a Week of Prayer worship talk at the Adventist Media Center a few years ago, and did some research in Ellen White's *Testimonies* on the topic of unity. I had plenty of quotes to choose from. Several great ones jumped out at me, and I picked out a favorite to use in my presentation. Leaving the open volume on my desk, I went to run a quick errand.

Returning a bit later, I planned to resume right where I left off. Although I didn't realize it, the pages in the open volume had flopped over to a completely different section of the book. Lo and behold, here was another passage, also on the topic of unity—and even more powerful than the first.

My point is simply that unity is one of heaven's great priorities. And it needs to be ours as well. "The unity of the church is the convincing evidence that God has sent Jesus into the world as its Redeemer" (*Testimonies*, vol. 5, p. 620).

Well, this is supposed to be a good news book. True, sin has the power to divide. But **humble, Christ-centered righteousness and unselfishness bring unity.**

When I gave that Adventist Media Center worship talk, I racked my brain to think of a personal example of how a person's obedience could bring this very unity. And I came up with one!

My older brother Dan and I both attended Far Eastern Academy out in Singapore. He was a sophomore and I was a freshman. For reasons that I really can't explain even to this day, Dan and I weren't very close during that period. He'd gotten there a year ahead of me and already had his circle of friends. Class loyalties were fierce, and *he* was in the class of '71. Nor were we roommates. Also he was short and I was shorter—which led to another problem. The entire male population of the school—and this was back in the days when guys always referred to each other by last names—fell into the unfortunate habit of calling him "Big Smith" and me "Little Smith." You can see why that would strain things a bit.

Don't get me wrong—there was nothing real ugly about it. We just didn't hang around with each other much.

One thing we did work on together, however, was the school paper, *Ripples*. He was an assistant editor and I wrote little "humor columns." They were shamefully stupid as I look back on them now. Not funny in any way that I can see, today they seem more like *anti*humor, as Dave Barry describes some of his failed jokes. But they pandered to the lowest common denominator, and back in those days the student population eagerly devoured any idiotic thing I chose to write about.

As it came time to hold student elections for the next school year, Dan announced his candidacy to be editor. Now, he was certainly qualified. After all, he'd done a great job working on the paper all year and had some well-thought-out plans for 1969-1970. In fact, he was so well prepared that he was running for the office unopposed.

Somebody on the election committee decided, at the last minute, that this was contrary to the spirit of democracy. "How about some write-in candidates?" the person suggested.

Well, a few of my less intelligent friends came up with an idea. "How about Little Smith?" Never mind that I was a baby-faced 13-year-old *and* stupid *and* unprepared. "Man, he's a funny guy! Let's do it! He can run against his brother. What a gas!" Some other students picked one of the junior girls as their candidate, and before you could blink, Dan faced a three-way race with Judy and Little Smith.

Snickering the whole way, I campaigned furiously for the job. I put up posters all over campus that read "Forget brotherly love. Vote for Little Smith!" I made sleazy campaigning a whole new Singapore art form. It was a contest that didn't just take the low road—it went clear into the ditch.

Well, there's really only one true thing you can say about voting populations—they are made up of fools. A whole segment of the student population at Far Eastern Academy decided to vote for Yours Truly as a joke. Plus I had promised them all cookies. When the ballots in the primary race were counted, Judy had come in first and I had come in second. My brother Dan, who was the only true candidate, found himself eliminated. Judy and Little Smith were the ones going into the final election.

All at once it hit me what a low thing I had done to my own brother. I knew two things in my heart: I was woefully unqualified. And I had treated my older brother shamefully.

How stupid could I have been? How could I have lent my squeaky, prepubescent voice to such a misguided effort? I felt sick—but it was too late for that. I didn't know what to do but feebly carry on and hope I would lose honorably to Judy in the general election.

Suddenly there came a knock on my dormitory room door. It was Dan.

As I stood there staring at him I knew I deserved the tongue-lashing of my life. That's for sure. But as long as I live I will never forget what happened next.

Dan stood there with a whole file folder of materials. Posters. Planning materials. Campaign ideas. "I'll help you all I can, David," he said simply.

And my heart almost stopped as I sat on the edge of my bed, aghast. I had sinned against my own brother—and here he was offering to help me win. He was willing to contribute ideas, to be *my* associate editor. Anything.

Let me tell you something. Things were different between me and Dan after that. Not immediately, but I can look back at that experience as a first step toward each other. Today we have unity between us. I would gladly do anything or go anywhere for my brother Dan.

There is a happy end to this story, I'm glad to say. The rules committee checked their bylaws more carefully and decided that Dan, the legitimate and declared candidate, should not lose his place in the field. Instead, he should run against the write-in candidate who got the most votes. That was Judy. Whew! Set free by a technicality!

Needless to say, I worked my tail off to get Dan elected. Going around to every foolish friend of mine, I told them Little Smith was going to thrash them personally if they didn't get me off the hook by voting for my brother. When the ballots were counted, Dan had squeaked into office by a single vote. And he went on to become one of the best editors Far Eastern Academy has ever had.

That's my story—of what one righteous act of love and forgiveness can do to real people and real relationships. I've seen the power of humble obedience, because it touched my own heart.

It's said that when a Christian has a willingness to serve rather than be served, great miracles can happen. When we set aside our human desire for supremacy, then the prayer of Jesus for unity in His church will be answered.

Steve Mosley has written a number of *It Is Written* scripts that point out how former bigots become brothers in Jesus. Ku Klux Klanners become ardent campaigners for racial justice. Republicans and Democrats learn to love each other. People with "attitudes" get over them. It's only the gospel of Jesus that can bring unity where division once reigned. "For he [Christ] is our peace, who has made us both one, and has broken down the dividing wall of hostility" (Eph. 2:14, RSV).

Just last week I was visiting with a friend who was reevaluating the place Jesus Christ should have in her life and in her marriage. I shared with her my amazement that *any* marriage survives without Christ at the core. It's only because of Jesus that a person can become capable of putting a spouse ahead of himself. (Not like the man who complained to his friends at work, "I'd have a great marriage if it weren't for my wife.")

I know that for Lisa and me, it's our commitment to Him that enables us to remain faithful to each other. He is the source of our unity. (More about that later.)

Earlier I mentioned the 1967 football season described by Green Bay Packer Jerry Kramer in his book *Instant Replay*. At times he would encourage his "party animal" teammates to cool it. In fact, "encourage" is probably too gentle a word. He would lean right into his carousing friends, all 245 pounds of him, and let them know that their actions of disobedience were jeopardizing everyone's chances of a Super Bowl victory. "You better lay off the girls before the games," he said to one very talented halfback. "You better get yourself some rest. You better give those girls some rest, too." He said it with a smile, but the kind of smile that's backed up by determined muscle. And for the world champion Packers, unity in obedience brought ultimate victory.

Of course, in a discussion of Adventist unity—especially that discovered "through obedience"—one string of questions really grips us. Who defines obedience? Unity on what topics? On what issues do we insist on victory, and where do we allow the "big tent" to exist?

Obviously, if everyone in Adventism would just be willing to see things my way, we'd have blissful unity at last. Unfortunately, a few misguided Adventists out there stubbornly refuse to go along with me. What then?

Despite my tongue-in-cheek moment, it is a sometimes overwhelming dilemma. We all cry for unity in the church. But some counter immediately that a unity achieved by acquiescing on their favorite point of debate is not unity, but a sellout. The first steps down the slippery slope to apostasy.

What points are really important, worth sacrificing unity for? Nobody can agree even on that. The late Walter Martin, in speaking about Christian controversies, had this slogan: "In essentials, unity; in nonessentials, diversity, and in all things, charity."

Fine and well. But what things are essentials? Martin, after all, headed up the Christian Research Institute, the world's best-known cult-watching group. A negative word from him could sweep an entire denomination into the kingdom of the cults. He told his readers what things were "essentials."

C. S. Lewis, in *Mere Christianity*, observed that "one of the things Christians disagree about is the importance of their disagreements. When two Christians of different denominations start arguing, it is usually not long before one asks whether such and such a point 'really matters,' and the other replies: 'Matter? Why, it's absolutely essential.'"

In our own Adventist Church right now we find countless debates on what people consider essential. Is the doctrine of the nature of Christ essential? How about abortion? Women's ordination? Perfection? The use of music performance tracks in church?

Ten or so years ago, when I was attending an Adventist church in the central coast region of California, a man left our local fellowship because the board decided to ordain women even as local elders. I pleaded with him to stay "for the sake of unity," but he would not. Fortunately, he found another Adventist church some 20 miles away and transferred his membership there. But I have no doubt that he would have left Adventism over the issue. To him, it was "essential."

Let me try to make several points, none of which will address the specifics of any of these issues here. I have opinions on all of them—please understand that. But nothing I say on this page or in the next decade could resolve a single one of these debated points. That in itself is perhaps a point.

First of all, live in obedience. Be an obedient Christian, faithful to the call of Christ in your own life. That's the point of this book, of course.

But I believe that the closer we are to Jesus Christ, the more we attune our lives to Him, the more we will find unity with one another. Will we reach "perfection of unity"? Not until He comes again. But obedience is a major step in the right direction.

When I teach the mathematical transitive property—"If $a = b$ and if $b = c$, then $a = c$"—I find in it a great application to Christianity. If I am close to the cross of Christ, and if my brother or sister is likewise close to the cross of Christ, we will naturally be close to each other.

It's possible that if some of those who are most actively promoting certain divisive causes in the church could kneel down and wash the feet of their antagonists (and vice versa), unity might result. If those who produce attack videos and send out their mailings could meet and pray and weep with the very conference leaders they're criticizing, perhaps heaven's transitive property could bring some unity to the church. At least it's a thought.

A second point, if I may. As I said, I *do* have opinions on almost all the issues rolling around in our denomination today. Women's ordination. The nature of Christ. Abortion. I could prepare a Smith position paper on each of them.

But nothing I can say or write will resolve these questions. One-on-one experience has shown me that. I've had friendly discussions with friends who disagreed with me. Even after two hours they still disagreed with me. We continued to love each other, but our views had not changed.

With that in mind, is it possible that we should now accept the inspired counsel to "press together"? Some issues simply are not resolvable on this earth. To continue endlessly to debate and to persuade the unpersuadable is a clear step toward division.

I think of recent General Conference sessions in which people formed long lines in order to get to the microphones to debate the question of women's ordination. On and on and on . . . and on and on. Pro arguments and con arguments. Perspectives from this field and that one. Texts and quotes tossed into the fray for both sides. Anecdotes that brought tears to your eyes—and they were on both sides.

The only thing that was perfectly clear was that agreement *was not* going to take place. The group as a whole simply was not going to vote a change. The church had no consensus, and it wouldn't have one anytime during the sessions.

I couldn't help wondering if the chair should have made an announcement: "Unless you have some *compelling new evidence or point to make* that you're convinced will persuade *this entire officially elected body*, may I ask you to be seated? Further discussion is simply bringing more disunity."

On some of these questions we are simply spinning our wheels, sinking ever further into ruts it will be hard to escape from.

Perhaps this is naive thinking—I don't know. But I'm encouraged by the response to a wonderful book by Marvin Moore entitled *The Crisis of the End Time,* in which he basically says the same thing. "All such divisive discussions must cease now."

A few years ago I had an informative breakfast visit with a woman who attended an Adventist church pastored by a close friend of mine. I had already heard that his church was experiencing the pain of a "split" over one particular theological issue.

She was gracious, but with real determinedness began to ask my opinion of the debate. Although I was a total stranger to her, she pulled a thick pile of papers out of her purse that contained many debate points and quotations to support her view of the issue.

We visited for 15 minutes or so, and I shared in what I hoped was a nonconfrontational way how the question appeared to me. But then I said, "I can tell this is very important to you. I mean, the fact that you have these materials with you in your purse would make me think that."

She nodded in agreement.

"Tell me," I went on. "This question has divided your church, hasn't it?"

Another nod.

"It's caused difficulty and even agony for your pastor, hasn't it? It's slowed down the mission of your church. Wouldn't you agree with me on that?"

She conceded that everything I had said was true.

"Obviously I don't know the answer to this particular theology you're concerned with," I admitted. "If a clear, compelling answer did exist, we as a church would likely have found it by now and moved on to other things." I took a breath. "But it's very clear to me that continued debate on this question, *and* your methods of dealing with it, **are being used by Satan to hurt the church.**"

The woman paled a little bit, but I will give her credit—she admitted that I might be right. And when I spoke with the pastor a few months later, he happily reported that she had become one of his staunchest allies in moving the church toward unity. Praise God!

Friend, it's perfectly all right to have views. What about the "nature of Christ"? Study it for yourself. Read up on the subject. Reading about Jesus is always a good idea. Form your own opinion. It's even all right to have friendly, Christ-centered discussions on it.

But permit others to do the same. Allow your neighbors and even your pastor to also be Bible students—without your insistence that they join you in all opinions.

We see a very special kind of righteousness wherever Christians learn to do this. Where grace and a trust in God's power to save others who still hold differing views temper passionate beliefs and opinions.

I'm slowly getting to the point where I trust God to save my evangelical friends. The young woman I had a Bible study with just last Friday is a beautiful Christian. She spoke earnestly about her love for Jesus. And I trust God to lead her into new truth in His own time and way. Maybe He will use me in that process—that would be wonderful. Right now she and I don't have the same perspective on the state of the dead and an eternal hell. Those are two big questions—I even think they're "essential." But the Holy Spirit is up to the task of taking care of things. I'm simply going to wait right here and be ready to say a loving word when the Holy Spirit prompts me.

So let's obey. Let's stay close to the cross. Let's trust God to resolve the unresolvable.

And one thing more: let's become like little children.

Someone once mused that "there are few problems in the church that wouldn't be fixed by people spending a few weeks in the cradle roll division of Sabbath school."

Go in there next Sabbath. If you're still mad about how the local conference is handling funds or if you can't see straight because of the "larger view" of atonement, then go to cradle roll. Watch the kids singing "The trees are gently swaying, *showing God is love!*"

I remember watching Karli in cradle roll when she was 2 years old. *She* didn't worry about the nature of Christ. Instead, she just knew He loved her! Perfection? Of course she wanted to be a good girl, because that made Jesus happy. How good could she be? Well, naturally she'd be as good as she could—God would be even happier with that. And why was she going to heaven real soon? 'Cause she loved Him so much.

It's all so easy down in cradle roll!

I watched them singing one Sabbath. "Let's play we are little frogs," the teacher said. "Hopping . . . hopping . . . hopping!" They hopped with delight up to the board to put their flannel froggies up next to a picture of Jesus. Karli gave me a toothy grin as she put hers closer to Jesus than anyone else's. Then the rest of the song: "Jesus loves little frogs. Hopping . . . hopping . . . hopping!"

Well, there's the gospel. Jesus loves little frogs—He loves us, too. What kind of "nature" does He have? Loving, it seems. So we love Him back. We obey Him because we love Him and want to make Him even happier.

Let me just note that the cradle roll attendees were in perfect, happy unity. As they hopped up to the board to get close to Jesus, they were cheerfully close to each other. "Except ye . . . become as little children . . ."

I must turn down a different alleyway now and observe that there *is* also a kind of unity that is dangerous. The followers of Sun Myung Moon seem to have more unity than just about anyone. In fact, sometimes 2,000 of them get married in one gloriously synchronized ceremony.

David Koresh's followers were unified in their devotion to him. Jim Jones's disciples had total harmony as they lined up to worship and drink their deadly potion at the feet of their chosen human leader. Hitler's millions shared in a rabid unity and loyalty to the führer.

Human history would seem to demonstrate that safe unity can be focused only on the Lord Jesus Christ. In my last book, *Watching the War,* I wrote about grand societies on unfallen planets—men and women who lead their worlds and are kings and queens to vast families. They are holy creatures, free-thinking men and women with minds and indomitable personalities far stronger than ours. Today and always, they have had free wills.

And they are in complete unity! "One pulse of harmony and gladness beats through the vast creation," Ellen White tells us. Because they have centered their lives, their very existence, on Jesus. They love Him supremely, and somehow that does the trick.

C. S. Lewis writes about a fleet of ships sailing toward the harbor. Each craft is seaworthy in itself, and all are heading toward the same place. So they have no collisions.

In my own life I'm finding that when we learn to love the Lord . . . and the people of the Lord . . . and also the church of the Lord—well, then we want to obey for the *sake* of that church. *Craving* unity, you'll sacrifice in order to help achieve it.

I try to remind myself often to cling to a "Calvary perspective." I want Calvary to grow and grow in my mind and in my life so that it just fills me up. And then I ask myself, "David, what argument, what feud, what little bit of angry resentment is worth hanging on to—in light of the cross of Calvary? What doctrinal debating point is worth grinding out? What enemy is worth hanging on to (as an enemy) when compared to the incomparable gift of Jesus on that cross?"

This is hard to do, and I guess that's why we're advised to spend an hour a day thinking about that cross. As Calvary grows in our lives, everything else will shrink.

Let me close with one final illustration. We as Adventist Christians are both challenged and discouraged by this well-known admonition: "Christ is waiting with longing desire for the manifestation of Himself in His church. When the character of Christ shall be perfectly reproduced in His people, then He will come to claim them as His own" (*Christ's Object Lessons*, p. 69).

I know these two sentences mark the gateway to a scarred battlefield, and it's one I don't wish to enter (for the reasons stated above). But consider this one humble application.

We all want to be like Jesus. For the sake of unity. Because of Matthew 5:16. In order to be His pillars. To help hasten His coming. And all the other reasons this book has described. (As well as other reasons that I'm sure are precious to you.) But it *is* discouraging to keep wondering if any *one* of us will ever be *perfectly* like Christ in every way.

Let me describe to you "the stadium card trick."

Sometimes before a big college football game or even a Super Bowl extravaganza, its organizers give out a series of huge colored cards to everyone in the stands—or at least to those chosen ones sitting in certain sections.

When the signal is given, each person holds up his or her assigned card. And the millions looking on via television from a Goodyear blimp see a perfect picture. A massive perfect picture of, say, a Dr. Pepper can of soda. But it could be anything. A new Chevy S-10 pickup. The school mascot. Even a beautiful portrait of Christ.

No, you're not creating that perfect picture alone. But sitting there in unity with everyone else, holding your card joyfully in the air as high as you can, you participate in the creation of that perfect picture.

In order for this to work, you have to be at your assigned place. You can't be out at the refreshment stand or taking a restroom break. Nor can you come late or leave early. Especially, you can't be out in the parking lot complaining and picketing.

Is it possible—and please don't make this a "doctrinal suggestion"—that as God's people experience unity and we each reflect the character of Christ by daily allowing the Holy Spirit to sanctify us, we can all be a part of a "global card demonstration"?

Onlookers, and even those viewing from unfallen worlds, might just glimpse the whole, complete character of Christ perfectly reproduced in *all* His people as we hold up the cards we've been given.

Don't write to me with your opinion. But think about it.

CHAPTER NINE

The God Who Gave Up

A few years ago Lisa and I drove over to the mall on a Sunday afternoon. For some reason I had gotten myself behind schedule, so I adopted a fairly aggressive driving attitude. It is a motoring philosophy one can learn in a city like Bangkok, where the vehicle code is one sentence long: "If you spot an opening—seize it!"

Meeting no serious challengers, I grabbed a parking spot and we headed indoors where it was air-conditioned. Several hours later I came out, only to find an angry note pasted to my windshield and written on a Pizza Hut napkin. Here's what it said:

"Listen, bud, you cut right in front of me and just about took off my front bumper. What's the matter with you?" And then the writer had added this chilling complaint: *How come the worst drivers in the world all have a 'Jesus Fish' on their car?*

Well, that was a sober drive back to the house. I mean, this guy had me. I was absolutely guilty on all counts—and with a "Jesus Fish" on the back of my Toyota the whole time. I spent a half hour trying to find a phone number for my anonymous writer, but never did track him down. Short of giving away free copies of this book to every registered driver living in southern California, I don't know how else I can say "I'm sorry." But believe me, I *am* sorry!

What we put on the bumpers of our cars means something!

Usually when people personalize their license plates, I don't "get" their cryptic messages. Lisa has to explain them to me. But bumper stickers are something else. A recent favorite said this: "I love animals." Then in smaller type right below that, it added, "They're delicious!" (It kind of looked like the conference president's car as it roared past me, but I couldn't be sure.)

But the most common one is "Please be patient." And you know how the rest of it goes. "God isn't finished with me yet."

Now, that is a good bumper sticker. Sanctification *is* the work of a lifetime.

But it would be too bad if we always drove the way I did to the mall that Sunday, speeding and swerving and clipping people's fenders and feelings, while sporting bumper stickers that said, "Sorry, folks. This is as good as it gets." In other words, *this is all God could do*.

Sometimes a hotel will put out signs: "Please excuse our mess." And we try to be forgiving when that happens. But the same sign shouldn't be there five years later. After a while you begin to wonder about that place's management.

This leads to our next observation about obedience:

Sinful living denies God's life-transforming power. Or victorious living *testifies* to His power.

Your obedient life says to a watching world, "This is what God can do! This is His handiwork." As already mentioned, most people can only judge God by His human ambassadors. It's no wonder many of them conclude, in the words of J. B. Phillips: "Your God is too small." If He even exists at all.

Earlier I mentioned my great admiration for the Bible hero, Moses, whose greatest concern in life was God's reputation. Moses winced—he *anguished*—as he thought of the onlooking nations watching the foolish antics of God's people. "For the sake of Your reputation, *do something!*" he pleaded.

It's in that same spirit that Joseph spoke firmly to the seductive Mrs. Potiphar, "How could I do something like this, and sin against God?"

Joseph had nothing to fear from STDs, pregnancy, or AIDS. No one was around to tell on him. In fact, a powerful and beautiful woman had made it clear that in this sex trap all the risks came in saying no.

But the heart of Joseph had a concern for God's image. Even as a hormone-packed teenager he somehow knew what Mrs. P would have probably thought *after* the bedroom party was over. "Well, he was easy. All this Jehovah talk is just that—talk. When push comes to shove . . ." And that would have been a fair conclusion on her part.

Whether I like it or not, when I flunk an algebra student, parents will wonder, "What kind of teacher is this guy?" When children grow up to be delinquents, everyone in town muses, "What sort of parents did they have? What sort of influence turned out a product so flawed as this?"

Art Buchwald (him again?) wrote a delightful piece back in 1964 about the Johnson-Goldwater election and all the subliminal strategies people were using to get their man elected. One fellow, a staunch Johnson man, would tip taxi drivers five cents and tell them, "Vote Republican!" Another Democrat spent all his spare time driving around D.C. cutting people off, honking his horn at them, and stealing their parking spots—in a car plastered with "Goldwater for President" stickers all over it. "I'll pick up most of my votes in late October," he told a friend, "when I accidentally stall on the Fourteenth Street bridge." A third described his tactic of going to elegant dinner parties, loudly announcing his support for Goldwater, and then spilling wine all over the host's new tablecloth.

Buchwald admitted that Republicans knew dirty tricks too. One man discovered a gimmick that he said worked miracles. He would pick people's names out of the phone book, call them up at midnight, and say, "I'm a volunteer for Johnson. Could you spare a few minutes?"

The point of Buchwald's humor is obvious: People would blame Goldwater and Johnson for the obnoxious behavior of these local yokels—which is precisely why they did it.

Michael Dukakis got booed for saying it in the 1988 presidential campaign, but it's sort of true that "a fish rots from the head down." A vicious campaign often has a vicious leader at the helm.

Candidates shrug off unethical lapses as being the work of an overzealous low-level staff member, but voters know better.

And so, like it or not, when Christians drive like maniacs, it reflects on our Leader. People assume that God hasn't the power to transform us into obedient and courteous motorists.

You can read stories in *Time* or even in the *Adventist Review* about doctrinal bickering. And innocent bystanders who look on wonder to themselves, *Who's the power behind that?* What else would you expect them to think?

We must at this point, then, "cut to the chase." Is it really solid Adventist/Christian theology that God will transform His people? Will we become good as we walk in the light? When we wear the wedding garment, is that our own goodness or simply the perfect character of Christ judicially and perpetually covering our naughtiness, our filthy rags?

I grew up in the Venden clan, so the famous "Wedding Garment" sermon is part of my heritage. (I have to be careful how much I borrow sermons from famous relatives. I heard of a preacher who began "borrowing" his way right through a particular book of sermons. Unfortunately, one of his parishioners had the same book . . . and soon picked up on the pastor's trail. One Sunday he offered congratulations. "Good sermon today, Pastor. And next week's is good too!")

Morris Venden describes the friend who offers us a Cadillac Seville or a Mercedes 450SL with *no down payment whatsoever*. Fantastic! Gimme the keys!

But hold on. A question explodes in our minds. And when we find out that the monthly payments are $1,000, we sadly conclude that we must turn down the free car. "I can't afford this 'free' gift. It's too expensive."

That is too often the discouraged Adventist's conclusion. "There's no hope for me. I would be glad that salvation is initially free, but there's no way I can be obedient enough starting with the day I'm converted. The monthly payments are just too steep."

One of the true folklore stories in the Smith family goes back to the year my mom presented my dad with a Macintosh computer that *she* wanted. It was her dream toy. And it was for *his* birthday! As far as anyone knew, he hated computers and never intended to use one. (To this day he still doesn't know how to turn it on.)

But we all watched as she presented it to him. An indescribable look flashed across his face as he spotted the Apple logo on the box. A brief moment of hope. "Maybe there's golf equipment inside." But no. He pulled out peripherals and disks and Mac manuals and all sorts of ugly start-up gear. You could tell that he despised it all. Happy birthday indeed.

The crowning blow—and perhaps the low point of their relationship that year—came when Mom told Dad that she had paid for *half* of his computer. Half a computer was her birthday present to him. If he would just cover the other half, everything would be fine. "Mom, maybe you'd better stay at our place tonight," I whispered to her out in the kitchen. (But things are OK now. She's used the computer, and he's used the story—as leverage in subsequent years.)

Is salvation just half a gift? With the impossible half being our responsibility?

I want to tell you about Ron. When I taught in an Adventist school, one year our tenth-grade geometry class had only three students in it. I decided to try an interesting experiment with them. "Anytime you want, we will set aside our geometry books and discuss spiritual things instead," I told them. "Anytime!"

It went great. Maybe once a week we would replace theorems and postulates with theology and prayer. All three kids still went on to get legitimate A's in the class, and we had some in-depth discussions along the way.

To this day I can't forget the spark of interest in Ron's eyes. He *wanted* to be saved. It was something he honestly longed for. But he just couldn't quite make the leap.

I appreciated the fact that we were close enough friends that he could concede he hadn't made the decision. I invited him to—many times. But he simply was not able to do it.

Why? Despite my repeated assurances, he was convinced that salvation was only a down payment—with the monthly payments totally up to him. "Hey, Mr. Smith," he would protest, waving his pencil in the air, "I know that as soon as I do it, I'd have to stop doing . . ." His voice would trail off. "Well, you know." Ron had a little list of things that he knew with certainty he was powerless to relinquish.

What theology do we have for that? Venden tells a similar heart-wrenching tale of the college girl who really wants to come to Jesus. Right now! "Well, why don't you?" asks a friend.

"I can't."

"How come?"

A painful pause. "I have plans for the weekend." And those plans involved a motel and a married man.

So, no thanks. Even though we like Cadillacs and we *want* a Cadillac and have always wished to drive one and have looked wistfully at others who seem to be happily driving them, we have to turn it down. Earning $1,000 a month to keep up those payments is something we just can't see working out.

Here is where we turn to Matthew 22. It's a simple story, and every Adventist knows it well. It tells of a wedding feast to which the invited guests don't bother to come, and so the host extends an open invitation to everyone. "Whosoever will." Good and bad alike, the Bible says. And soon riffraff and assorted sinners fill the Hilton Hotel banquet hall.

The king comes in to look over the guests. To "investigate" them, Venden says. There is a judgment of some kind, apparently. And one man is there without the royal robe on. He has no good answer when pressed on the question. So he gets cast out into darkness, where there is weeping and gnashing of teeth.

This is where my friend Ron chimes in. "See? I can't make it! I can get in the front door, but I can't stay there."

But what do the puzzle pieces represent? The invitation—issued freely to all—is the gift of justification. Because of Calvary, everyone gets invited. So far so good.

The robe of righteousness, the robe of obedience—what about it? Ellen White tells us that it represents the process of sanctification, the obedience of the saints, the righteousness of Christ *worked out in the lives of God's believers.* Revelation 19:8 says it really is *them being good.* "By the wedding garment in the parable is represented the pure, spotless character which Christ's true followers will possess" (*Christ's Object Lessons*, p. 310).

And so my friend Ron's shoulders sag in despair. The college girl with a motel key in her pocket sadly turns away. They have the wedding invitation, but that spotless robe of righteousness—they can't do it.

And this is the point in the sermon where my uncle Morris Venden's voice breaks with emotion. **"But the robe is just as free as the invitation. Even the robe is a gift from the King!"**

He goes on to add that he wishes he could find a thousand ways to shout it from a thousand rooftops for all the Rons of the world to hear. The robe of Christ's righteousness—*worked out in our lives*—is God's gift to us. Obedience is *given* to those who daily walk with Jesus. Justification is free. Sanctification is free. Everything's free. Jesus seems to be able to do it all! God provides the down payment . . . and the monthly payments . . . and the insurance payments . . . and takes care of the oil changes every 3,000 miles. Everything!

Christ's Object Lessons goes on to declare: "This robe, woven in the loom of heaven, has in it not one thread of human devising" (p. 311).

I guess this section in the book links back to chapter one. We can't do it except by God's power. Our obedience has got to come from Him. Some who are stronger than geometry student Ron and his teacher David Smith can *pretend* to obey in their own strength. But real sanctification, a real fine-linen wedding robe, can only come from the King.

My NIV study Bible makes this conclusion in a footnote: "It may have been the custom for the host to provide the guests with wedding garments. . . . The wedding garment no doubt speaks of the righteousness that God, the gracious host, provides for all who accept his invitation. God issues an undeserved invitation to undeserving people, *and in addition provides the righteousness the invitation demands.*" What a God!

Hebrews 13:21 describes how God will "equip you with everything good for doing his will, and may he work in us what is pleasing to him, through Jesus Christ, to whom be glory for ever and ever" (NIV).

I vividly remember sitting in an academy Bible class and hearing that justification is God's job and sanctification is ours. The teacher drew a wavy line going up and up and up, indicating that the better we became, the less we would need God. It was the explicit "subsidy religion" I mentioned in chapter one.

Please understand that I'm not complaining. God brings us into truth when we are ready for it. And grace—the life-transforming *totality* of grace——is an exceedingly hard doctrine to fully grasp.

The very same week that I shared these messages in the young adults division at the Wisconsin camp meeting, I was also asked to give some worship talks in the earliteen tent. One evening I asked the kids there to define the word "grace." And really, out of about 15 young people, I didn't hear a single *workable* definition that approached the spirit of "unmerited favor." Nothing even close.

This isn't meant to be an indictment of our pastors and our teachers and leaders. I honestly believe that the devil is masterful at simply blocking out this truth every time we hear it. More than any other, "grace" is the one signal he has successfully scrambled because it is so contrary to fallen human nature.

So we must get to where we never tire of hearing it! I don't mind if our pastors preach on grace and sanctification 52 times a year. I want to hear as many camp meeting sermons on this as I possibly can. "The robe is just as free as the invitation!"

In early 1995 our *Voice of Prophecy* program presented two weeks of sermons built on the gospel song "Amazing Grace." We found a beautiful sermonette in every single phrase of just the first stanza. "Amazing grace! how sweet the sound, that saved a wretch like me! I once was lost, but now am found, was blind, but now I see." That's eight sermons right there, and we need 800 of them before we're even getting started. "When we've been there ten thousand years . . ."

So maybe it's true, as one book title suggests, that it's "hard to be lost." Look at all God has done. He's provided the invitation (free) and also the robe (free). God gave us Calvary, sent us the Holy Spirit, and poured out His providential workings, His miracles, His leading.

Hey, there's more. He's given us the writings of Ellen G. White. And godly friends who guide and strengthen us and pray with us and for us. Many of us have been blessed with devout parents who have wrestled in the prayer closet for *decades* on our behalf.

Yes, it is hard to be lost. No wonder Paul exclaims in Romans 8 that we are "more than conquerors" (verse 37, NIV). He then adds: "For I am convinced that neither death nor life, neither angels nor demons, neither the present nor the future, nor any powers, neither height nor depth, nor anything else in all creation, will be able to separate us from the love of God that is in Christ Jesus our Lord" (verses 38, 39, NIV).

Having said that, we must concede there are some things God can't do. And, strangely enough, I'm even glad for that.

He can't make us be saved. And that is good news—for everyone in the universe. It's hard to be lost—but not impossible.

God can call to us. He can beckon and tug on our sleeve, can pour out His miracles. The Lord is an active, not passive, loving Father. But we have to accept both the invitation and the robe. It *is* possible to turn both of them down.

You can be *invited* to church—but you still have to get up and finally go there. No one will thrust you, protesting, into the prayer closet. God never forces anyone.

A Sabbath school friend of mine once complained that he wished that God would flash a lot more power. And we had quite a spirited debate, wondering whether we really wanted a God who overpowered us, who either forced or dazzled us into helpless compliance.

But how much more attractive is the kind of God it turns out we do have! He lays the options out for us and compellingly tells us how much He wants us. Then He shows us that He can and will take on the task of transforming us.

Finally *we* decide.

So, what is our focus? To get with Christ . . . and allow the results to happen.

I said it to my friend Ron. And to this day it causes me anguish that it didn't register. "Ron, just take Him right now! And those battles you're worried about—let that be His responsibility. He will *give* you obedience in His own time and way."

With the gift of both the invitation and the robe comes assurance! Perfection of character can only happen as we realize that we're accepted all along the way.

Martin Weber tells a delightfully insightful story about a person who faces a $25,000 fine if he doesn't fall asleep (obey) by 10:00 p.m. Twenty-five thousand bucks? If I'm not asleep (obedient) by 10:00?

Of course, that announcement would give you such a case of jitters that sleep (obeying) would become impossible. Your mind would be lurching over the dreaded consequences and screaming out the telephone numbers of Adventist loan sharks.

But suppose someone said, "Dave, the fine's off. Forget about that part. Get some rest."

Ahhhhh . . . and you know what? You'd be asleep (obedient) in eight minutes. Freed from the pressure of rejection and punishment, you would find joy in obeying.

Morris Venden summarizes it all in 15 words: **The entire basis of the Christian life is in knowing Jesus as a personal friend.** The invitation *and* the robe both come from that one activity. It's the only way *real* transforming—from sinners into model drivers—happens.

Does it really work? Believe me, I've tried it both ways—and this is the way that does work. I wish it worked faster, though. Ellen White tells us we'll never feel like we're growing as much as we should. We'll often have to bow down and weep and confess our shortcomings, but we're not to be discouraged. Jesus doesn't cast us off.

I remember a convention speech by Jesse Jackson in which he spoke of his empathy with those in America who struggle against formidable odds. "I understand," he said. "I know. I may be running for president now, but I have had your experience." And I've had enough of a glimpse of what we're talking about in this chapter to know that it works and that I want much more.

Does God have a plan? Yes! Does He have the power to carry out that plan? Yes! "Shall we go on sinning?" Paul asks (Rom. 6:1, NIV). No! God has a plan. He has a plan for you!

The God Who Gave Up

At our Thousand Oaks Adventist Church we like to sing a song that declares that our God is an awesome God who reigns with wisdom, power, and love.

Wisdom—and power—and love. A God with only two out of the three would not be much of a deity. He might even be a monster. Thankfully, we have a God with all three attributes. He *does* have the power to transform our lives. Another song we sing describes Him as Lord of the power enabling us "not to sin."

Whenever we find ourselves confronted with Satan's power, we can remind ourselves that the devil is mighty, but Jesus is *almighty*.

Just a few weeks ago I again began to read through volume 1 of *Testimonies for the Church*. It is a tough and gritty book. But you find in its remarkable author a transformed life. God showed through her what He could do. Despite doctrinal differences, even her most bitter critics have lauded the holy life of Ellen G. White. By common consent, we can agree that here was a person who had allowed God to give her a robe of righteousness.

You've likely read how even D. M. Canright, who left the Adventist faith and viciously attacked her visions as fraudulent, still attended her funeral. He stood at the side of her casket with tears rolling down his cheeks. "There is a noble woman gone," he wept.

The late Walter Martin, author of *Kingdom of the Cults*, gave the Adventist Church a "clean bill of health" largely because of the influence of Ellen White. "Her writings characterize her as a sanctified Christian in every sense of the word," he wrote.

And Kenneth Samples, who in 1994 authored *Prophets of the Apocalypse*, a book about the Waco tragedy, praised the godly woman who led Adventism ever closer to orthodox Christianity. He described our denomination as the only one born in the nineteeth century that developed such a trend. "For this, it is Ellen G. White who must be commended."

The testimony of a transformed life carries great weight!

In fact, Ellen White herself "stayed the course" after the Great Disappointment for two reasons. First, no one had refuted William Miller's math. But second, and far more important, was this argument found in *The Great Controversy*: "The fruits of the advent movement, the spirit of humility and heart searching, of renouncing of the world and reformation of life, which had attended the work, testified that it was of God" (p. 405).

Lives had been changed—and this gave a teenager named Ellen confidence that God was with the fledgling Advent movement.

I've decided to slow down and drive more carefully.

CHAPTER TEN

Helping the Dodgers Win

A quiz question flashed on the scoreboard at a major league baseball game one evening. "Someone *in the ballpark tonight* has played for every National League team. Can you name the person?"

Well, people in the stands went nuts trying to guess the answer. Who in the world had played for *everyone*? You could see people scratching their heads and comparing notes.

An inning later they flashed the answer: "The stadium organist."

Now, that is one crippled joke! But it contains a measure of truth.

The organist at Dodger Stadium has, in a sense, played for the Dodgers. Not just "played music." Nancy Bea Heffley has actually participated in Dodger wins by the way she has performed.

After every L.A. home run she plays a celebration tune followed by a long drum roll that rumbles through the stadium. During Dodger rallies her fanfares and "Charge!" renditions have whipped up the L.A. faithful until the stadium was rocking. Don't tell me she's not responsible for some Dodger runs.

But the Los Angeles Dodger organization has another secret weapon that few people know about. Until now, that is. I'm so mad at them for the 1994 strike that I'm going to blow their cover right here.

My daughter Kami.

It is absolutely incredible what that girl has done for the Dodgers in recent years. And it's all so simple. She simply goes to games.

For some twilight zone reason the Dodgers virtually *always* win when Kami is there. She and I calculated once that over the stretch of about four years L.A. was something like 35 and 4 in games in which she was at the ballpark. They enjoy a better than 80 percent win-loss percentage with Kami Lyn Smith in attendance.

And this is largely during a period when the Dodgers were a less than wonderful team. Even in seasons when they were well under .500 as a club, they would win six out of seven if Kami showed up.

Often, right before a game I would see manager Tommy Lasorda come out of the Dodger dugout and scan the upper deck, an anxious look on his face. But when he spotted Kami and me sitting up in the red seats, a relaxed smile would cross his face. I'd see him go back into the dugout and whisper something to the players, pumping his fist in satisfaction. Sure enough, they'd pull it out.

(Skeptics may question the above paragraph, but that's how I remember it.)

Sometimes in the middle of an extended losing streak, when Kami and I were sitting at breakfast, I would tell her: "Lasorda called here this morning before you got out of bed. I think he was crying. *Begging* you to come to tonight's game. What do you think?"

What a feeling of power to know that you control a team's destiny that way! I've thought of suggesting to the Dodgers that they give her (and me) season tickets.

I have tried other combinations too, especially after Kami went away to college. Karli and I are not bad—about a .650 pairing. Pastor Rob Randall and I went to seven games in three years—and never saw the Dodgers lose. In 1994, before the strike, they won six in a row for me no matter whom I went with to the ballpark.

Hey, maybe *I'm* the lucky one!

(On the other hand, many years ago I took the Valley View Adventist Academy choir to three Dodger games. They lost by scores of 2-0, 4-0, and 13-1. By common consent I was released from that teaching assignment.)

It's a well-acknowledged fact in sports that fans play a part in the victory. I mean, in basketball the hoops are at a height of exactly 10 feet for both teams. But "home court advantage" spikes the winning percentage for virtually every team in the NBA. Sure, part of it is the familiar surroundings and the home cooking and the fact that players can go home and see their families each night. But the cheers of the crowd and the organ-enhanced chant "Thump—Thump—DEE—fense! Thump—Thump—DEE—fense!" is part of why a team wins at home.

I'll never forget being at Candlestick Park one Sunday afternoon with 57,000 fans cheering for Mike Ivie during an at bat against the Dodgers. When Ivie hit a grand slam, there came a wall of sound that had *terrifying* power.

Many baseball clubs refer to their supporters as "the tenth player" and mention this when giving out RVs, free airline tickets, and toaster ovens on Fan Appreciation Day. It's a public acknowledgment that fans are actually participants in a team's success. They have played a role in that team's victory. At the very least, the money we've paid in for tickets has helped them to buy the necessary millionaire players so that they can win. (What a comforting thought.)

All of this brings us to the final reason—and, I believe, one of the best and most rewarding—for our obedience: **Righteousness helps bring about the final victory.**

For nine chapters we've been considering how our faithfulness helps to strengthen the church. How it draws others in. How it brings honor and glory to God. How it enables the Holy Spirit to unleash His power.

And our obedience—yes, *always* a gift from God—helps to defeat the enemy's claims that God's people can't learn to love righteousness.

All of these reasons rolled together spell victory. Actually, they spell *participation* in a victory already won. But we are helping! For our sakes, God has allowed us to participate in this greatest of campaigns.

In *Watching the War* the unfallen king and queen of Senteria accompany God and the Son to a virgin earth. Malachon and Pershia meet the wide-eyed first couple of the new world. God then explains to Adam and Eve why He has allowed the presence of Lucifer on earth. Then Pershia makes a breathless little speech, urging the newly created humans to be faithful to God.

" 'It will not seem as easy as you perhaps think.' The Son's voice held a note of warning. 'To separate the two of you, then to deceive, will be Lucifer's strategy.'

" 'Please!' Pershia's voice burst out despite her reserves. 'It sounds simple. Then let it be so!' She looked from one to the other. 'Adam. Eve. Already I feel you are my brother and my sister. Already I love you!'

"They nodded, their eyes fastened upon hers. 'And we you.'

" 'Listen to me, then!' She leaned forward. 'Whatever it takes— stay true to the Three. Malachon and I, we have served our God faithfully for many years. We and our world so far away in Senteria.' A huskiness crept into her voice as she thought of her children and grandchildren so far away. 'To obey and love God is more joy than beings can almost bear. Wonderful, unspeakable happiness. Why risk it on Lucifer's empty promises? Please, I beg you, for the happiness of the universe . . . stay true to God. Love Him as we do.'

"The rush of words ended in a little gasp. Slightly embarrassed, she lapsed into silence.

"The Son smiled and stood with a laugh of delight. 'Pershia, Pershia.' He laid a loving hand upon her shoulder, then traced her noble cheek with His fingers. 'That was a fine speech.' Glancing at Adam and Eve, He repeated, 'A fine speech.' "

You know, I almost don't think it *is* science fiction anymore. God is looking at this very moment for people who will love Him with that kind of intensity—joyously obeying out of a fervent devotion, as the queen of Senteria has described here. A fierce and intense conviction that God is wonderfully *right*.

Let me say again that we are participants and combatants in a great and marvelous cause. The great controversy is, in a very real sense, a good controversy struggle because it is a defense of God. It is a victory that will last.

I used to think that the most important thing in the world was for me to get to heaven. Now I realize that the number one issue in the universe is **God winning this war.** Would you agree with that?

And we can wake up every morning and sense the Spirit calling us to the war theater. We get to participate! And some of the greatest battles since Calvary are going to be fought right now.

A wrenching war story has a mortally wounded soldier lying in an army hospital bed thousands of miles from home. He stirs, conscious for just a moment, and realizes his probable condition. But he manages to whisper the question to the nurse. "Miss . . . , am I going to die?"

The young girl winces, but then slowly nods her head. It is too important a moment for cheap lies.

For just a moment he sighs, then nods, accepting the situation. "Well, that's what I came here for."

This is not to say that we must die in the war—although some surely will. But good soldiers are glad to participate in the battle, whatever the cost, because they know they are involved in something bigger than themselves. A higher principle is at stake.

We are now to the point where I can risk telling you about my yellow postcard.

Back in late 1992, when I had just accepted the position as president of the Religious Public Relations Council, I wrote a letter to Little Rock, Arkansas, on RPRC stationery. It was the day after the November election, and I expressed congratulations to Clinton and Gore, wishing them well in their new, God-ordained responsibilities in leading the republic.

As expressed earlier, I'm a very fair-minded fellow whose political leanings are a complete secret. I'd have sent a similar letter to Bush/Quayle if they'd won, but they didn't. So there.

A couple months later I received a yellow postcard in the mail. And this is what the *handwritten* message said:

"Thanks so much for your support and encouragement. With your help, we can change our country and put our people first."

It was signed "Bill."

Bill! I had a postcard from Bill!

The 146 Republicans at the Adventist Media Center fell all over themselves trying to explain to me that the postcard had come out of a laser printer somewhere in the bowels of a huge office building in Little Rock. President-elect Clinton hadn't written it himself, they said. But I found their arguments weak and unpersuasive as well as tinged with jealousy. After all, the postcard had been received by *me*, not them. And it was *handwritten*. That's proof.

It was right during this time that a new expression popped into vogue: FOB. Certain people around the country were suddenly "friends of Bill."

How did a person become a friend of Bill? Well, if you had gone to Little Rock High School, that was one way. Or if you had roomed with Clinton at Oxford. Or if you played the saxophone. Your best chance was if you owned a McDonald's franchise anywhere in the state of Arkansas or within a 50-mile radius of Washington, D.C. That was rumored to be a sure ticket to a Supreme Court nomination.

And I'm sure many people across America muttered in frustration after the election, "I sat two tables over from the guy in the cafeteria in high school. I could have shared my Twinkies and my Hostess Ding Dongs with Bill, but I didn't. Now it's too late!"

In the rough-and-tumble years that have passed since then, I've often thought about what a "friend of Bill" is expected to do. What is his or her role? Why does a president need friends?

President Nixon, in contrast, did not seem to seek many "friends of Richard." In fact, the story's told that on election night in 1968, when Nixon was triumphing over Hubert Humphrey, one of his friends turned to the president-elect and said, "Well, congratulations, Dick."

The newly elected leader's face hardened. "That's 'Mr. President' to you." The icy chill of leadership.

Nixon didn't seem to need friends. At the former president's 1994 funeral a stoic Spiro Agnew sat in silence, alone with his thoughts. It was reported that he and Nixon had had no contact with each other following the vice president's resignation in 1973.

What about God? In His great final cosmic political campaign, why has He sought out friends? Why does He want us as participants in the great war so many in the universe are watching?

Is there such a thing as an FOG? A "friend of God"? We've talked about people such as Enoch and Abraham. In these 1990s, is God looking to expand His kitchen cabinet?

I've always liked the verse in John in which Jesus looks around at the 12 disciples and invites them to be part of this inner circle. "I no longer call you servants, because a servant does not know his master's business. Instead, I have called you friends, for everything that I learned from my Father I have made known to you" (John 15:15, NIV).

Can you imagine it? "I want you," Jesus says. "I don't just want your vote—I want you as friends. *Close* friends! I need you in My administration as confidants and advisers. I want you on My cabinet. I've got to have you as key players in this ultimate campaign."

In January of 1994 I attended the National Religious Broadcasters convention in Washington, D.C. One evening I just missed seeing the president at a nearby hotel where he had met with all the Democratic governors. People in tuxedos and evening gowns were scurrying around, picking up their wraps and going out through the security gates.

All at once a long motorcade went by, the red strobe lights flashing in the cold night air. And then a huge blue limousine. There they were in the back!

I was tempted to wave my yellow postcard (I keep it in my suit pocket, close to my heart at all times) at Clinton and see if he'd pull over and visit. Surely he'd remember! But the Secret Service was all over the place, and it was late. I was tired—surely he was tired too—so I let the procession pass.

A few moments later a conservatively dressed woman passed me on the sidewalk, going the other direction. "Did you see the president go by?" I asked her, trying to keep my voice from quivering.

She gave a little shrug. "Well, I see him all the time."

I gulped. "Oh." It seemed like a bad time to brag about my postcard. "You're kidding. How come?"

"I'm his AIDS policy director."

Sure enough, it was Kristine Gebbie, walking home after the banquet. Policy czar for the nation's AIDS program, she was a frequent visitor to the Oval Office. A certified "FOB."

I've been thinking since then about what a friend of Bill does for his or her president. The phenomenon has some wonderfully challenging lessons for us to inculcate into our own lives as we determine to be radical disciples and friends of God.

First and obviously, a friend of the president helps to get his or her candidate elected. You'll do anything to get the person into the White House. Chuck Colson, who carried it to an extreme, said he would "drive over his grandmother" if he had to in order to get Nixon another four years. George Stephanopoulos, it's reported, spent the six months before election 1992 working without a single day off, helping Clinton. Eighteen hours a day, seven days a week, for six straight months. Not a single day of vacation or Sabbath rest.

An FOB also assists in getting the president's agenda passed. The new administration's legislative priorities become the person's own passion. Whether you work in Washington or simply represent the chief executive's interests in Smallville, U.S.A., where you live, you are a tireless representative for the Magna Carta of your leader. A new crime bill, a better budget, a health care plan, a campaign ethics package—they are *your* concerns too, when you're a friend of the president.

We as Seventh-day Adventist Christians have taken on the mandate of Matthew 28 as part of our agenda. "Therefore go and make disciples of all nations, baptizing them in the name of the Father and of the Son and of the Holy Spirit, and teaching them to obey everything I have commanded you" (verses 19, 20, NIV). As friends of God, this is what we're determined to do. God's dreams are our dreams.

Second, a "friend of Bill" is on duty 24 hours daily to defend the president's reputation. He or she speaks out against all attackers, discrediting the false rumors and lies that may swirl around us. The president's spin doctor is willing to appear on *Meet the Press* and *This Week With David Brinkley* and *Face the Nation*—all on the same Sunday.

Why? In defense of the president! "Our president is not the kind of man these rumors are making him out to be," he or she declares. "I know the president. I was in that meeting. I have the evidence right here in these transcripts. These reports are scurrilous—they're from an enemy."

What a challenge for the friends of God to do likewise!

Helping the Dodgers Win

A friend of the person in the Oval Office is also responsible to talk up the president at every opportunity. Always! You don't take time off when you're an FOB—you don't burrow behind a book or a magazine, hoping to be left alone. No, you seek out every chance to say a word on behalf of the administration.

I'm sure that if I sat next to Leon Panetta or some other member of Clinton's cabinet on a long airline flight, we wouldn't end up talking about the Baltimore Orioles or the latest soap opera. No, a president's men and women seize every conversational opening—and testify about the president and his plans!

You know, I always admire those Christians who seem to take every conversation and graciously steer it toward the things of God. Not in a contrived and dopey way that kills the party, but with class and attractive conviction. H.M.S. Richards, Sr., was such a man. He had a two-word slogan: "Jesus only." Every sermon and every sidewalk visit seemed to flow inexorably toward the things of the Saviour. It didn't matter where you started. One could always predict where it would end: "Jesus only." God needs such people whose focus is on Him.

Here's another point: a friend of the president is willing to do whatever he or she gets asked to do despite personal preferences. If the president needs you to take on this or that job, you do it. You serve at the leader's pleasure.

You may recall how in 1992 President Bush needed James Baker to run his flagging reelection campaign. Now, Baker had the plum job in the whole administration—he was a capable and successful secretary of state. Staying where he was was a sure ticket to even higher ambitions.

On the other hand, the election drive was sputtering. He might or might not be able to save the day. Polls were cementing fast, with Bush/Quayle trailing.

If he'd had his druthers, Baker would have said, "Forget it." Why jump on board the *Titanic?* Far better, from a personal point of view, to stay above the fray and keep flying around the globe to important foreign capitals to meet important foreign leaders. Let Bush lose—and then make your own presidential move in 1996.

But James Baker was a "friend of George." He was the president's man. Of course he would do what he was asked to do. To his credit, he took the job at the election committee and gave it all he had. He served where he was needed.

Are we willing to be God's friends—no matter what that commitment may mean? Moving away? New job responsibilities? Mission service in desolate lands? A high post or a low one, in prosperity or in poverty? Praise God for the many FOGs who have done great things in obedience to the call of the Master!

And now the best FOG characteristic of all . . .

To be the friend of the president is the number one element of your life.

When you work for Him, that is what you *are*. That's your identity. You don't answer people by saying, "Well, let's see. My name's Dave. I have a nice wife and two kids. I'm a big Dodger fan, and I went to PUC and my favorite show's *The Simpsons* and I love tortilla-chip casserole and pralines-and-cream ice cream. And, oh yeah—by the way, I have a job working for the president of the United States."

No, your status as a friend is the number one thing in your life. That's it! That's what you are—it's what you become. You truly do grow into a radical disciple.

Chuck Colson, in his book *Born Again,* describes the harried pace in the White House during the Watergate years. Months went by without a letup. He simply could not get away for any vacation. Finally he and his wife, Patty, did manage to slip off and fly down to Florida for a desperately needed break. Mentally fatigued almost beyond belief, he set up a lawn chair and prepared to enjoy a few hours of gazing out at the Atlantic Ocean.

Just then the phone rang. The White House operators, legendary for their ability to track down anybody, anyplace, anytime, had caught up to him. "The president needs you back." Some new Watergate pot had boiled over. A new crisis had arisen that only the president's favorite hatchet man could tame.

This isn't to imply that being God's man or woman will always be a frenzied, nail-biting kind of job. But it illustrates the kind of commitment God is looking for. Do we make our loyalty to Him our total identity? Is our place in His Oval Office of supreme importance in our lives?

We must observe that it's possible to be a friend of the president—and then leave. The nation found itself amazed during the closing years of the Reagan administration at how many close friends departed the administration to write bitter "kiss and tell" books. You can leave—the back door of the White House has no lock on it.

But those who stay are transformed. The friends who are faithful to the end are not the same afterward.

Is it something you are willing to say yes to? Because the yellow postcard is coming to your home right now. Not a phony laser-printed announcement spit out by some impersonal Hewlett-Packard printer. God's invitation is real, and it comes from the highest office in the universe.

The stakes are high when the president calls you. Ever thought about that? "Dave, I need you. We're tackling big things: the deficit, world turmoil, the crises in Rwanda and Bosnia, the threats to our religious liberties. You're the one I need."

How could you say no?

David Gergen, senior editor of *U.S. News and World Report* and a registered Republican, received such a call from President Clinton. The White House staff desperately needed the insights and solid management ability that only Gergen could provide. Would he come on board? Would he leave his coveted spot in academia and join the fragile Clinton team?

Gergen did. The need was so great that he could not turn down his president.

Think of getting a message from Abraham Lincoln. "I need you. We've got to lick this slavery thing. We've got to preserve the union. Mary Todd and I feel you're the only person who can help us do it." You'd *have* to say yes. The stakes are just too high.

And how high are the stakes in this spiritual war we are in? The war that so desperately needs our obedience and loyalty? It is the biggest campaign ever conceived. The Commander in Chief has already sent out the notices. He needs us! And not for four or eight years, but for eternity.

I'm getting excited just thinking about it.

May I observe here that a group of people like the "friends of Bill" is generally a small group. It's not a vast, teeming army. No, it's rather small, an inner circle.

Is the same true with God?

You might protest: "David, there are 8 million Adventists. The broader Christian realm contains multiplied hundreds of millions more. It may have started with 12, but it's not small now."

All true. And yet—when you think about those who are as committed to God as Chuck Colson was to Nixon, those who are radical disciples, those who have made friendship with God their number one identity—*that* is a small group. God's circle of close friends—of trusted confidants—is not very large.

A few years ago I was teaching a college algebra class at the local community college. It was a big group, about 40 students. One evening during the break I began chatting casually with some of them about their religious backgrounds. They already knew mine, so it was a natural point of discussion.

To my amazement, I found that *not one out of 40* had any kind of church experience at all. None of them. I was the only one. We talk about "dark countries" and even "dark counties." Those expressions have real meaning. Some people have worked for God in areas in which they were the only ones representing Him. A lone candle in the inky spiritual darkness. What a rare privilege!

You know, I have always loved the beautiful way C. S. Lewis has of describing God's people, His committed followers. Lewis pictures them as quiet, solid people who have found the lasting joy that comes from obedience. His word portraits of these rare people fill me with a sense of intense desire.

Listen to this poignant testimony from his book *Mere Christianity*. It appears in the chapter "The New Men."

"Already the new men are dotted here and there all over the earth. Some, as I have admitted, are still hardly recognizable: but others can be recognized. Every now and then one meets them. Their very voices and faces are different from ours; stronger, quieter, happier, more radiant. They begin where most of us leave off. They are, I say, recognizable; but you must know what to look for. They will not be very like the idea of 'religious people' which you have formed from your general reading. They do not draw attention to themselves. You tend to think that you are being kind to them when they are really being kind to you. They love you more than other men do, but they need you less.

. . . They will usually seem to have a lot of time: you will wonder where it comes from. When you have recognized one of them, you will recognize the next one much more easily. And I strongly suspect (but how should I know?) that they recognize one another immediately and infallibly, across every barrier of color, sex, class, age, and even of creeds. In that way, to become holy is rather like joining a secret society. To put it at the very lowest, it must be great *fun*."

Those words are chillingly beautiful, aren't they? The new men and the new women filled with quiet joy. In all of life, they are never really beaten down. While there are not too many of them, they still dot the landscape. And they recognize one another as friends of God.

I say again, I would love to get the invitation to be one of them. What a privilege it would be, what an exciting and breathtaking honor! To be invited to serve, to be a part of this greatest of campaigns.

Have you ever had a long shot at the dream job—but your chances were slim? "I'd give *anything!* Please!" And then the phone call comes.

Friend, this is the position we find ourselves in. God wants us! The long-awaited call has come through. Do you believe it?

You and I can decide to be a part of this dream team, the ultimate inner circle. Our joyfully obedient lives can count toward God's final victory.

Maybe it's ironic that after 10 chapters of grappling with such big thoughts and quoting such learned authors, we should end with a bit of philosophy from a cartoon dog named Snoopy. But that's what we're going to do.

In an old, old strip, Snoopy the beagle is watching as various kids traipse past—Charlie Brown and Lucy and Schroeder and all the others.

And Snoopy thinks to himself: *I wonder why some of us are born people and some of us are born dogs? Why is that?*

Some more kids run past as his mental soliloquy continues. *I mean, is it just chance? Or fate? A cosmic accident? Some are people . . . and some are dogs.* The question has him in a state of deep reflection.

Finally he cocks his head and observes: *Somehow it doesn't seem quite fair. Why should I have been the lucky one?*

Friends of God. Why should we have been the lucky ones? I don't know.

But we are.